TEN LESSONS OF ARABIC

TEN LESSONS OF ARABIC

based on

Das Sabaq of Mawlana 'Abd al-Salam Kidwai Nadvi

Revised by
'Aamir Bashir

Copyright © Dār al-Saʿādah Publications 2011
First Online Edition Dec 2011
Second Online Edition Jul 2012

ilmresources.wordpress.com

"General and unrestricted permission is granted for the unaltered duplication, distribution, and transmission of this text."

In Plain English: Make as many copies as you want.

TABLE OF CONTENTS

Table of Contents		i
List of Tables		ii
Acknowledgments		iii
Foreword		v
LESSON 1	مُبْتَدَأٌ وَخَبَرٌ – Subject and Predicate	1
LESSON 2	مُضَافٌ وَمُضَافٌ إِلَيْهِ	7
LESSON 3	اَلْفِعْلُ الْمَاضِيْ – Past Tense Verb	11
LESSON 4	فِعْلٌ، فَاعِلٌ، مَفْعُوْلٌ – Verb, Subject, Object	19
LESSON 5	اَلْحُرُوْفُ الْجَارَّةُ – Prepositions	25
LESSON 6	اَلضَّمَائِرُ – Pronouns	31
LESSON 7	اَلْفِعْلُ الْمُضَارِعُ – Present and Future Tense Verb	39
LESSON 8	اَلصِّفَةُ وَالْمَوْصُوْفُ – Adjective	49
LESSON 9	اَلْأَمْرُ وَالنَّهْيُ – Imperative & Prohibitive	57
LESSON 10	اَلْوَاحِدُ، اَلتَّثْنِيَةُ، اَلْجَمْعُ – Singular, Dual, Plural	67

LIST OF TABLES

3.1	Past Tense Verb Forms in Active Voice (اَلْفِعْلُ الْمَاضِيْ الْمَعْرُوْفُ)	12
3.1a	اَلْفِعْلُ الْمَاضِيْ الْمَعْرُوْفُ	13
3.2	Past Tense Verb Forms in Passive Voice (اَلْفِعْلُ الْمَاضِيْ الْمَجْهُوْلُ)	14
3.2a	اَلْفِعْلُ الْمَاضِيْ الْمَجْهُوْلُ	15
5.1	Prepositions (اَلْحُرُوْفُ الْجَارَّةُ)	25
6.1	Unattached (مُنْفَصِلٌ) Pronouns	31
6.2	Attached (مُتَّصِلٌ) Pronouns	32
7.1	Verb Forms of (فِعْلٌ مُضَارِعٌ) in Active Voice (مَعْرُوْفٌ)	39
7.1a	اَلْفِعْلُ الْمُضَارِعُ الْمَعْرُوْفُ	40
7.2	Verb Forms of (فِعْلٌ مُضَارِعٌ) in Passive Voice (مَجْهُوْلٌ)	41
7.2a	اَلْفِعْلُ الْمُضَارِعُ الْمَجْهُوْلُ	42
9.1	Creating Second Person Imperative In Active Voice (أَمْرٌ حَاضِرٌ مَعْرُوْفٌ)	58
9.2	Second Person Imperative in Active Voice (أَمْرٌ حَاضِرٌ مَعْرُوْفٌ)	58
9.2a	اَلْأَمْرُ الْحَاضِرُ الْمَعْرُوْفُ	59
9.3	Creating Second Person Prohibitive (نَهْيٌ حَاضِرٌ مَعْرُوْفٌ) in Active Voice	60
9.4	Second Person Prohibitive (نَهْيٌ حَاضِرٌ مَعْرُوْفٌ) in Active Voice	60
9.4a	اَلنَّهْيُ الْحَاضِرُ الْمَعْرُوْفُ	61
10.1	Singular, Dual, and Plural	68

ACKNOWLEDGMENTS

I owe a debt of gratitude to many people who helped in making this project a success. To begin with, I would like to thank Sr. A. Naviwala who, working on behalf of Darul Uloom al-Madania, prepared the first draft, which I edited. I would also like to thank Mawlana Ibrahim Memon for his valuable feedback. I am also indebted to my First year students at Darul Uloom (2011–2012 academic year) who suggested important improvements and pointed out the many mistakes. My prepatory year students at Darul Uloom (2011–2012), including Ahmad Hatim who proof-read the draft for the second edition, have also given me valuable feedback. I have greatly benefitted from their questions, comments and suggestions. May Allah reward them, and all others for their contributions and help.

بسم الله الرحمن الرحيم والصلوٰة والسلام على رسوله الكريم

FOREWORD

This is the second edition of the revised *Ten Lessons of Arabic*, which in turn was based on the famous Urdu language primer of Arabic grammar *Das Sabaq* [Ten Lessons] by Mawlana 'Abd al-Salam Kidwai Nadvi. *Das Sabaq* in Urdu has been a part of the *'Aalim* course curriculum in Western *madrasahs* for a number of years. In 2011, I was commissioned by Darul Uloom al-Madania to edit a translation that they had prepared by revising an existing translation of the text that was available online. I completed the editing in a few months. During this process, I took liberty with the translation to make the content more accessible and beneficial to the student. The edited version was then used as a textbook for Darul Uloom's eAlim program. At that time, I received a number of suggestions from eAlim instructors and students regarding improvement of the text.

Later, I got the chance to teach the first four chapters myself during Ramadan 2011 to a sincere student. At that time, I realized the many flaws that had remained, especially in the first four chapters. I revised these chapters thoroughly to make them more student friendly. Later still, I got the chance to go over the whole text during the first term of 2011–2012 academic year, while teaching it to first year students at Darul Uloom. During this time, a number of issues came up and I made the changes accordingly. The first online edition was released at that time.

Later, during the last two terms of 2011–2012 academic year, I got the chance to teach it again; this time, to the prepatory year students at Darul Uloom. More issues came up and I fixed them. Now, at the end of this academic year (2011–2012), I have gone through the whole text again and revised it throughly. I have added more explanation and tables in many chapters. I have also revised the word lists and exercises, and reduced the overall number of vocabulary words. While teaching, I had felt that memorizing too many new words was taking the students' attention away from the real thing, viz. grammar rules and construction of the language. In many cases, plurals of words are given, but they are merely for reference. Students should not be required to memorize these. The vocabulary lists still appear quite formidable. However, this is because of the many repeated words. If they were to be taken out, the overall count will be much less.

This text has been revised multiple times. In the process, it has changed considerably and those looking for an exact translation of *Das Sabaq* will be disappointed. However, I believe it is now much more beneficial. I have tried my best, with help from many of my students, to remove all of the errors in it. Nevertheless, as is the case with all human endeavors, there are bound to be some mistakes in it, and definitely, room for improvement. I hope that the readers, students and teachers, will apprise me of any such issues. Your feedback (suggestions, constructive criticism, etc.) is valuable to me. You can contact me at the email address given at the end.

This is a beginner-level text but notwithstanding its ease, it should be studied with a teacher. It is also expected that the student will be studying other Arabic books along with it as well. I would recommend *Fundamentals of Classical Arabic* vol. 1 (by Dr. Husain Abdul Sattar) and *Durus al-Lughah al-'Arabiyyah* vol. 1 (by Dr. V. Abdur Rahim). I got the chance to teach both during this academic year. They are both excellent books. There is some overlap between them and *Ten Lessons*. However, this should not be seen as redundancy, but as re-inforcement. Of the three, *Fundamentals* is for *Sarf*, *Ten Lessons* and *Durus al-Lughah* are for general Arabic. The last one is probably the best in terms of its gradual and progressive introduction to Arabic language concepts. However, the former two provide concise information for *Sarf* and *Nahw*, which is spread out in *Durus al-Lughah*. I recommend that *Ten lessons* and *Durus al-Lughah* be started at the beginning of the semester, while *Fundamentals* be started in the second half.

Since this is a beginner-level text; therefore, Arabic words have not been transliterated exactly, keeping in mind that most people at this stage will not be comfortable with Arabic transliteration schemes. Rather, their approximate equivalents have been used that are easier to read for the untrained. Nevertheless, non-English words have been italicized.

As for duals and plurals of Arabic words, the original Arabic duals and plurals have not been used; rather, their plurals have been created the English way by adding an 's' to the singular. Thus, two *dammahs* is used instead of *dammahtain*. The word still remains italicized to reflect its non-English origin.

The following abbreviations appear in the text:

S = Singular   D = Dual   P = Plural
M = Masculine   F = Feminine

Many times, these have been used in combination. Thus, we also have the following abbreviations:

(S/M) = 'Singular masculine' which means one male
(D/M) = 'Dual masculine' which means two males
(P/M) = 'Plural masculine' which means multiple males
(S/F) = 'Singular feminine' which means one female
(D/F) = 'Dual feminine' which means two females
(P/F) = 'Plural feminine' which means multiple females

I hope and pray that this revised edition will be of benefit to the students. I also pray that Allah Most High accepts this humble effort from all those who have contributed to it in any way, and gives us the power to continue with more. I also request the readers and all those who benefit from it in any way to remember us all in their prayers.

And He alone gives success.

وَصَلَّى اللهُ تَعَالَى عَلَى خَيْرِ خَلْقِهِ سَيِّدِنَا وَمَوْلَانَا مُحَمَّدٍ وَعَلَى آلِهِ وَأَصْحَابِهِ أَجْمَعِيْنَ

'Aamir Bashir
Buffalo, NY
19th Sha'ban, 1433 (9th July, 2012)
Email: ainbay97@yahoo.com

LESSON 1

مُبْتَدَأٌ وَخَبَرٌ
Subject and Predicate

Consider the following sentences: 'Mahmood is knowledgeable,' 'Haamid is pious,' 'Khalid is a conqueror.' These sentences and other sentences of the same pattern are called *mubtada* (مُبْتَدَأٌ) and *khabar* (خَبَرٌ). The subject of the sentence is called *mubtada* and it comes at the beginning of the sentence. The predicate of the sentence is called *khabar* and it is the second part of the sentence. For example, in 'Mahmood is knowledgeable,' Mahmood is the subject and the information about him being knowledgeable is the predicate. Therefore, 'Mahmood' is *mubtada* and 'knowledgeable' is *khabar*.

To translate a sentence of this type into Arabic, follow these steps:
1. Take out the "is".
2. Translate the words into Arabic.
3. Give two *dammahs* (ضَمَّتَيْنِ) to both words in the sentence.

Examples:
1. Mahmood is knowledgeable.
   مَحْمُوْدٌ عَالِمٌ
2. Haamid is pious.
   حَامِدٌ صَالِحٌ
3. Khalid is a conqueror.
   خَالِدٌ فَاتِحٌ
4. Muhammad (Allah bless him and give him peace) is a messenger.
   مُحَمَّدٌ (صَلَّى اللهُ عَلَيْهِ وَسَلَّمَ) رَسُوْلٌ
5. Naasir is a friend.
   نَاصِرٌ صَدِيْقٌ

In the above examples, the *mubtada* is a definite noun.[1] However, if it is a common noun, an *alif-laam* will be added to the beginning of the word. For example, if the first sentence was 'the man is knowledgeable,' it would be translated as اَلرَّجُلُ عَالِمٌ.

It is important to note here that whenever *alif-laam* comes before a word, the *tanween* becomes a single *fathah* (فَتْحَة), *kasrah* (كَسْرَة) or *dammah* (ضَمَّة) as the case

---

[1] In Arabic, a definite noun is called *ma'rifah* (مَعْرِفَة) and a common noun is called *nakirah* (نَكِرَة).

may be, eg. رَجُلٌ becomes اَلرَّجُلُ. *Alif-laam* is mainly used in place of the definite article "the." It gives distinction to a word. For example, 'a man' is any man and 'the man' is a specific man. Sometimes *alif-laam* is used for the meaning of 'a whole category/class.' For example, اَلْإِنْسَانُ means 'mankind' and اَلْحَمْدُ means 'all praise.'

If the *mubtada* is feminine, then the *khabar* will also have to be feminine. To change a word to its feminine form, add the round *taa* (ة) to the end of the word. For example, 'the man is pious' is written as اَلرَّجُلُ صَالِحٌ. Now if you want to say 'the woman is pious,' you will say اَلْمَرْأَةُ صَالِحَةٌ. Similarly, 'the girl is knowledgeable' will be written as اَلْبِنْتُ عَالِمَةٌ.

Word List

English	Arabic	
	Singular	Plural
father	أَبٌ	آبَاءُ
mother	أُمٌّ	أُمَّهَاتٌ
son	اِبْنٌ	أَبْنَاءُ
boy	وَلَدٌ	أَوْلَادٌ
daughter, girl	بِنْتٌ	بَنَاتٌ
paternal uncle	عَمٌّ	أَعْمَامٌ
paternal aunt	عَمَّةٌ	عَمَّاتٌ، عَمَّاتٌ
maternal uncle	خَالٌ	أَخْوَالٌ
maternal aunt	خَالَةٌ	خَالَاتٌ
brother	أَخٌ	إِخْوَانٌ، إِخْوَةٌ
sister	أُخْتٌ	أَخَوَاتٌ
grandfather	جَدٌّ	أَجْدَادٌ
grandmother	جَدَّةٌ	جَدَّاتٌ
grandson	حَفِيدٌ	أَحْفَادٌ، حَفَدَةٌ
granddaughter	حَفِيدَةٌ	
man	رَجُلٌ	رِجَالٌ
woman	اِمْرَأَةٌ	نِسَاءٌ

English	Arabic	
	Singular	Plural
male child, infant, toddler	طِفْلٌ	أَطْفَالٌ
female male child, infant, toddler	طِفْلَةٌ	
strong	قَوِيٌّ	أَقْوِيَاءُ
weak	ضَعِيْفٌ	ضُعَفَاءُ
ice, snow	ثَلْجٌ	
cold	بَارِدٌ	
water	مَاءٌ	مِيَاهٌ
sweet	عَذْبٌ	
small	صَغِيْرٌ	
fat	سَمِيْنٌ	
pious	صَالِحٌ	صُلَحَاءُ
worshipper	عَابِدٌ	عُبَّادٌ
intelligent, smart	ذَكِيٌّ	أَذْكِيَاءُ
	عَاقِلٌ	عُقَلَاءُ
hard-working	مُجْتَهِدٌ	مُجْتَهِدُوْنَ
beautiful	جَمِيْلٌ	
thankful, grateful	شَاكِرٌ	شَاكِرُوْنَ
truthful	صَادِقٌ	صَادِقُوْنَ
Lord	رَبٌّ	
prophet, messenger	نَبِيٌّ	أَنْبِيَاءُ
messenger	رَسُوْلٌ	رُسُلٌ
path	صِرَاطٌ	
straight	مُسْتَقِيْمٌ	
Muslim	مُسْلِمٌ	مُسْلِمُوْنَ
man, mankind	اَلْإِنْسَانُ	
slave	عَبْدٌ	عِبَادٌ
leader, commander	قَائِدٌ	قُوَّادٌ، قَادَةٌ

Lesson 1

English	Arabic	
	Singular	Plural
brave	شُجَاعٌ	
generous	كَرِيمٌ	كِرَامٌ
the hour; day of resurrection	اَلسَّاعَةُ	
coming (F)	أتِيَةٌ	
respectful	مُؤَدَّبٌ	
and	وَ	
merciful	رَحِيمٌ	
going (M)	ذَاهِبٌ	
knowledgeable; scholar	عَالِمٌ	عُلَمَاءُ

Exercise 1:   Translate into Arabic.

1. Haamid is a father.
2. Mahmood is a son.
3. Khalid is an uncle (paternal).
4. Zayd is an uncle (maternal).
5. Bakr is a brother.
6. Sa'eed is a grandfather.
7. Hameed is a grandson.
8. The man is strong.
9. The child (M) is weak.
10. The ice is cold.
11. The water is sweet.
12. The son is small.
13. Hamzah is fat.
14. The brother is pious.

Exercise 2:   Translate into Arabic.

1. The woman is strong.
2. The mother is beautiful.
3. The daughter is a worshipper.
4. The aunt (maternal) is intelligent.
5. The aunt (paternal) is hard-working.
6. The sister is beautiful.
7. The grandmother is thankful.

8. 'Aishah is intelligent.
9. Fatimah is small.
10. Maimoonah is a grand daughter.
11. The aunt (paternal) is pious.
12. The girl is fat.
13. The grandmother is pious.
14. The aunt (maternal) is a worshipper.

<u>Exercise 3:</u>   Translate into English.

1. اَللهُ رَبٌّ
2. مُحَمَّدٌ (صَلَّى اللهُ عَلَيْهِ وَسَلَّمَ) نَبِيٌّ
3. اَلرَّسُوْلُ صَادِقٌ
4. اَلصِّرَاطُ مُسْتَقِيْمٌ
5. مَحْمُوْدٌ مُسْلِمٌ
6. اَلْإِنْسَانُ عَبْدٌ
7. خَالِدٌ قَائِدٌ
8. اَلْقَائِدُ شُجَاعٌ
9. سَعِيْدٌ أَخٌ
10. اَلْخَالُ عَاقِلٌ
11. اَلْأَخُ كَرِيْمٌ
12. اَلسَّاعَةُ آتِيَةٌ
13. عَمْرٌو مُجْتَهِدٌ
14. طَارِقٌ مُؤَدَّبٌ
15. اَلْبِنْتُ مُؤَدَّبَةٌ
16. اَلْعَمُّ ذَكِيٌّ
17. اَلْحَفِيْدُ مُؤَدَّبٌ وَالْجَدُّ رَحِيْمٌ
18. فَاطِمَةُ ذَاهِبَةٌ
19. حَامِدٌ ذَاهِبٌ
20. مَحْمُوْدٌ عَالِمٌ

LESSON 2

مُضَافٌ وَمُضَافٌ إِلَيْهِ

Consider the following sentences: 'slave of Allah,' 'messenger of Allah,' 'door of the house,' 'the Messenger's order,' 'Mahmood's pen,' 'Khalid's book,' 'Hameed's house.' These phrases and those with a similar pattern are called *mudaaf* (مُضَافٌ) and *mudaaf ilayhi* (مُضَافٌ إِلَيْهِ). One thing (*mudaaf*) is attributed to the other (*mudaaf ilayhi*). Many times, the relationship is that of the possessed to its possessor. The possessed is called *mudaaf* and the possessor is called *mudaaf ilayhi*. For example, in the phrase 'Mahmood's pen,' the pen is owned by Mahmood. Therefore, 'pen' is *mudaaf* and 'Mahmood' is *mudaaf ilayhi*.

To translate a sentence of this type into Arabic, follow these steps:

1. Take out 'of' or the apostrophe and the 's,' which show possession.
2. If you have taken out the apostrophe and the 's,' reverse the sequence. Write the second word first and the first word second. If you took out 'of,' then there is no need to reverse the sequence.
3. Replace the English words with their Arabic equivalents.
4. Give the *mudaaf* a single *dammah* and the *mudaaf ilayhi* two *kasrahs*.

For example, to translate the phrase 'Mahmood's pen' to Arabic, first take out the apostrophe and 's.' It becomes 'Mahmood pen.' Then, change the order of the words to 'pen Mahmood.' Next, replace the words with their Arabic equivalents. You get قلم محمود. Now, give the *mudaaf* a single *dammah* and the *mudaaf ilayhi* two *kasrahs*. You get قَلَمُ مَحْمُودٍ. Following the same method, 'Khalid's book' becomes كِتَابُ خَالِدٍ. For a sentence with 'of,' such as 'ring of gold,' first remove the 'of.' It becomes 'ring gold.' Now, replace the words with their Arabic equivalents. You get خاتم ذهب. Now, give the *mudaaf* a single *dammah* and the *mudaaf ilayhi* two *kasrahs*. You get خَاتَمُ ذَهَبٍ.

The rules concerning *alif-laam* have been mentioned in the first lesson. Those rules will apply here also. Thus, if there is an *alif-laam* at the beginning of the *mudaaf ilayhi*, the two *kasrahs* will become one *kasrah*. خَاتَمُ ذَهَبٍ will become خَاتَمُ الذَّهَبِ. It should be noted here that the *mudaaf* never accepts *alif-laam* or *tanween*. For instance, in the above example, خَاتَمُ will not accept *alif-laam* or *tanween*.

Lesson 2

Word List

English	Arabic	
	Singular	Plural
wall	جِدَارٌ	جُدُرٌ، جُدْرَانٌ
home, house	دَارٌ	دِيَارٌ، دُوْرٌ
	بَيْتٌ	بُيُوْتٌ
door	بَابٌ	أَبْوَابٌ
window	شُبَّاكٌ	شَبَابِيْكُ
room	حُجْرَةٌ	حُجُرَاتٌ
	غُرْفَةٌ	غُرَفٌ
roof	سَطْحٌ	سُطُوْحٌ، أَسْطُحٌ
ceiling	سَقْفٌ	سُقُوْفٌ
bed	سَرِيْرٌ	سُرُرٌ
pen	قَلَمٌ	أَقْلَامٌ
heat	حَرٌّ	
sun	شَمْسٌ	شُمُوْسٌ
day	يَوْمٌ	أَيَّامٌ
judgment; religion	دِيْنٌ	
to establish, establishing	إِقَامَةٌ	
ritual prayer (*salah*)	صَلَاةٌ، صَلوةٌ	
to give, giving	إِيْتَاءٌ	
poor due (*zakah*)	زَكوةٌ، زَكَاةٌ	
city, town	بَلْدَةٌ	
country; city, town	بَلَدٌ	بِلَادٌ، بُلْدَانٌ
city, town	مَدِيْنَةٌ	مُدُنٌ
people		نَاسٌ
light	ضَوْءٌ	أَضْوَاءٌ
lamp	سِرَاجٌ	سُرُجٌ
darkness	ظُلْمَةٌ	ظُلُمَاتٌ

8

English	Arabic	
	Singular	Plural
night	لَيْلٌ	
finger, toe	إِصْبَعٌ	أَصَابِعُ
foot; leg	رِجْلٌ	أَرْجُلٌ
tall, long	طَوِيلٌ	
leader, governor	أَمِيرٌ	
short	قَصِيرٌ	
expensive	ثَمِينٌ	
high	رَفِيعٌ	
winter	شِتَاءٌ	
summer	صَيْفٌ	
spring	رَبِيعٌ	
autumn, fall	خَرِيفٌ	
new	جَدِيدٌ	
old	قَدِيمٌ	
book	كِتَابٌ	
note-book	كُرَّاسَةٌ	
jouney, travel	سَفَرٌ	

Exercise 1:   Translate into Arabic.

1. Haamid's son/son of Hameed
2. Khalid's mother/mother of Khalid
3. Fatimah's sister/sister of Fatimah
4. The house's wall/wall of the house
5. The room's door/door of the room
6. The room's window/window of the room
7. The house's roof/roof of the house
8. The room's ceiling/ceiling of the room
9. Hameed's bed/bed of Hameed
10. The grandfather's pen/pen of the grandfather
11. The sun's heat/heat of the sun

Lesson 2

Exercise 2:   Translate into English.

1. يَوْمُ الدِّيْنِ
2. إِقَامَةُ الصَّلَاةِ
3. إِيْتَاءُ الزَّكَاةِ
4. نَاسُ الْبَلْدَةِ
5. ضَوْءُ سِرَاجٍ
6. ظُلْمَةُ اللَّيْلِ
7. أَصَابِعُ رِجْلٍ
8. قَلَمُ حَامِدٍ
9. سِرَاجُ خَالِدٍ
10. أَمِيْرُ الْمَدِيْنَةِ

Exercise 3:   Translate into Arabic.
1. Mahmood's pen is expensive.
2. The house's wall is long.
3. The house's roof is high.
4. Haamid's son is tall.
5. Fatimah's sister is short.
6. Days of Summer are long.
7. Days of Winter are short.
8. Door of the house is high.
9. Ceiling of the room is expensive.

Exercise 4:   Translate into English.

1. اِبْنُ الرَّجُلِ عَاقِلٌ
2. بِنْتُ الْاِمْرَأَةِ طَوِيْلَةٌ
3. بَابُ الْبَيْتِ جَدِيْدٌ
4. أُمُّ مَحْمُوْدٍ قَصِيْرَةٌ
5. كِتَابُ عَائِشَةَ قَدِيْمٌ
6. كُرَّاسَةُ آمِنَةَ جَدِيْدَةٌ
7. بَيْتُ حَمِيْدٍ قَدِيْمٌ
8. اِبْنُ خَالِدَةَ ذَكِيٌّ
9. صَلَاةُ السَّفَرِ قَصِيْرَةٌ

LESSON 3

اَلْفِعْلُ الْمَاضِيْ
Past Tense Verb

In this lesson, we will look at the various forms a past tense verb takes in accordance with the number and gender of the one(s) performing the action. To begin with, it should be noted that فَعَلَ means "he (S/M) did," فَعَلَا means "they (D/M) did," فَعَلُوْا means "they (P/M) did," فَعَلَتْ means "she (S/F) did" and so on. These verbs are in active voice (فِعْلٌ مَعْرُوْفٌ).

In Arabic, each verb form is called صِيْغَةٌ (*seeghah*). Looking at the table below, we can see that there are fourteen *seeghah*s in it. Each of these *seeghah*s has a name. This name identifies, whether it is singular, dual or plural, whether it is masculine or feminine, and whether it is first person, second person or third person. In Arabic, the words for singular, dual and plural are وَاحِدٌ, تَثْنِيَةٌ, and جَمْعٌ, respectively; first person is called مُتَكَلِّمٌ, second person is called حَاضِرٌ, and third person is called غَائِبٌ; and masculine is called مُذَكَّرٌ, and feminine is called مُؤَنَّثٌ. Thus, singular masculine of the third person will be called وَاحِدٌ مُذَكَّرٌ غَائِبٌ in Arabic. Dual masculine of the third person will be called تَثْنِيَةٌ مُذَكَّرٌ غَائِبٌ, and plural masculine of the third person will be called جَمْعٌ مُذَكَّرٌ غَائِبٌ, and so on.

In the case of the first person, because the gender is not identified, and there is no separate *seeghah* for dual, therefore, the two *seeghah*s, singular first person and plural first person will be called وَاحِدٌ مُتَكَلِّمٌ and جَمْعٌ مُتَكَلِّمٌ, respectively.

Lesson 3

We are listing below the verb forms (also called conjugations) of the past tense verb in active voice. These should be memorized with their meanings.

Table 3.1
Past Tense Verb Forms in Active Voice (اَلْفِعْلُ الْمَاضِى اَلْمَعْرُوْفُ)

Person	Gender	Plurality	English	Arabic
Third Person (غَائِبٌ)	Masculine (مُذَكَّرٌ)	Singular	He did.	فَعَلَ
		Dual	They did.	فَعَلَا
		Plural	They did.	فَعَلُوْا
	Feminine (مُؤَنَّثٌ)	Singular	She did.	فَعَلَتْ
		Dual	They did.	فَعَلَتَا
		Plural	They did.	فَعَلْنَ
Second Person (حَاضِرٌ)	Masculine (مُذَكَّرٌ)	Singular	You did.	فَعَلْتَ
		Dual	You did.	فَعَلْتُمَا
		Plural	You did.	فَعَلْتُمْ
	Feminine (مُؤَنَّثٌ)	Singular	You did.	فَعَلْتِ
		Dual	You did.	فَعَلْتُمَا
		Plural	You did.	فَعَلْتُنَّ
First Person (مُتَكَلِّمٌ)	Masculine/Feminine	Singular	I did.	فَعَلْتُ
	Masculine/Feminine	Dual/Plural	We did.	فَعَلْنَا

Before we move on, it would be useful to see how Table 3.1 would be written in Arabic. This is as follows:

Table 3.1a
اَلْفِعْلُ الْمَاضِي الْمَعْرُوْفُ

اِسْمُ الصِّيغَةِ	اَلصِّيغَةُ
وَاحِدٌ مُذَكَّرٌ غَائِبٌ	فَعَلَ
تَثْنِيَةٌ مُذَكَّرٌ غَائِبٌ	فَعَلَا
جَمْعٌ مُذَكَّرٌ غَائِبٌ	فَعَلُوْا
وَاحِدٌ مُؤَنَّثٌ غَائِبٌ	فَعَلَتْ
تَثْنِيَةٌ مُؤَنَّثٌ غَائِبٌ	فَعَلَتَا
جَمْعٌ مُؤَنَّثٌ غَائِبٌ	فَعَلْنَ
وَاحِدٌ مُذَكَّرٌ حَاضِرٌ	فَعَلْتَ
تَثْنِيَةٌ مُذَكَّرٌ حَاضِرٌ	فَعَلْتُمَا
جَمْعٌ مُذَكَّرٌ حَاضِرٌ	فَعَلْتُمْ
وَاحِدٌ مُؤَنَّثٌ حَاضِرٌ	فَعَلْتِ
تَثْنِيَةٌ مُؤَنَّثٌ حَاضِرٌ	فَعَلْتُمَا
جَمْعٌ مُؤَنَّثٌ حَاضِرٌ	فَعَلْتُنَّ
وَاحِدٌ مُتَكَلِّمٌ	فَعَلْتُ
جَمْعٌ مُتَكَلِّمٌ	فَعَلْنَا

Note: In the tables above, فَعَلَ has been translated as "he did" and فَعَلَتْ as "she did." It should be kept in mind that these forms could also mean "it (masculine) did" and "it (feminine) did," respectively. The same is true of other forms. The masculine could be any masculine thing or person, and the feminine could be any feminine thing or person.

Lesson 3

Changing Active Voice to Passive Voice

Now, to change these verbs into passive voice, follow the following procedure. Put a *dammah* on the first letter (ف) of فَعَلَ, and a *kasrah* on its second letter (ع). It will become فُعِلَ. Its meaning will change to "he (S/M) was done upon." This is passive voice (فِعْلٌ مَجْهُوْلٌ). Similarly, فَعَلَا will become فُعِلَا, فَعَلُوْا will become فُعِلُوْا, فَعَلَتْ will become فُعِلَتْ, and so on. We are listing below the verb forms (also called conjugations) of the past tense verb in passive voice. These should be memorized with their meanings.

Table 3.2
Past Tense Verb Forms in Passive Voice (اَلْفِعْلُ الْمَاضِى الْمَجْهُوْلُ)

Person	Gender	Plurality	English	Arabic
Third Person (غَائِبٌ)	Masculine (مُذَكَّرٌ)	Singular	He was done.	فُعِلَ
		Dual	They were done.	فُعِلَا
		Plural	They were done.	فُعِلُوْا
	Feminine (مُؤَنَّثٌ)	Singular	She was done.	فُعِلَتْ
		Dual	They were done.	فُعِلَتَا
		Plural	They were done.	فُعِلْنَ
Second Person (حَاضِرٌ)	Masculine (مُذَكَّرٌ)	Singular	You were done.	فُعِلْتَ
		Dual	You were done.	فُعِلْتُمَا
		Plural	You were done.	فُعِلْتُمْ
	Feminine (مُؤَنَّثٌ)	Singular	You were done.	فُعِلْتِ
		Dual	You were done.	فُعِلْتُمَا
		Plural	You were done.	فُعِلْتُنَّ
First Person (مُتَكَلِّمٌ)	Masculine/ Feminine	Singular	I was done.	فُعِلْتُ
	Masculine/ Faminine	Dual/ Plural	We were done.	فُعِلْنَا

اَلْفِعْلُ الْمَاضِي

Again, before we move on, it would be useful to see how Table 3.2 would be written in Arabic.

Table 3.2a
اَلْفِعْلُ الْمَاضِي الْمَجْهُولُ

اِسْمُ الصِّيْغَةِ	اَلصِّيْغَةُ
وَاحِدٌ مُذَكَّرٌ غَائِبٌ	فُعِلَ
تَثْنِيَةٌ مُذَكَّرٌ غَائِبٌ	فُعِلَا
جَمْعٌ مُذَكَّرٌ غَائِبٌ	فُعِلُوْا
وَاحِدٌ مُؤَنَّثٌ غَائِبٌ	فُعِلَتْ
تَثْنِيَةٌ مُؤَنَّثٌ غَائِبٌ	فُعِلَتَا
جَمْعٌ مُؤَنَّثٌ غَائِبٌ	فُعِلْنَ
وَاحِدٌ مُذَكَّرٌ حَاضِرٌ	فُعِلْتَ
تَثْنِيَةٌ مُذَكَّرٌ حَاضِرٌ	فُعِلْتُمَا
جَمْعٌ مُذَكَّرٌ حَاضِرٌ	فُعِلْتُمْ
وَاحِدٌ مُؤَنَّثٌ حَاضِرٌ	فُعِلْتِ
تَثْنِيَةٌ مُؤَنَّثٌ حَاضِرٌ	فُعِلْتُمَا
جَمْعٌ مُؤَنَّثٌ حَاضِرٌ	فُعِلْتُنَّ
وَاحِدٌ مُتَكَلِّمٌ	فُعِلْتُ
جَمْعٌ مُتَكَلِّمٌ	فُعِلْنَا

Note: In these two tables, فُعِلَ has been translated as "he was done" and فُعِلَتْ as "she was done." As mentioned above in the note after Tables 3.1 & 3.1a, these forms could also mean "it (masculine) was done" and "it (feminine) was done," respectively. The same is true of other forms. The masculine could be any masculine thing or person, and the feminine could be any feminine thing or person.

Lesson 3

Creating Conjugation Tables from وَاحِدٌ مُذَكَّرٌ غَائِبٌ

Having memorized these two tables, the next stage is to identify the verb forms of other verbs by comparing them to these tables. For this, we need to know that وَاحِدٌ مُذَكَّرٌ غَائِبٌ of any verb table is considered to be the basic verb form. Generally, it is composed of three letters. The first is called فَاءِ كَلِمَةٌ, the second is called عَيْنِ كَلِمَةٌ, and the third is called لَامِ كَلِمَةٌ. Now all that remains to be done is to identify which letter of the new verb matches which letter of the basic verb form of the tables given above. Consider, the verb نَصَرَ (he helped). Comparing this to فَعَلَ of Table 3.1 or Table 3.1a, we can see that in this verb, ن is the فَاءِ كَلِمَةٌ, ص is the عَيْنِ كَلِمَةٌ, and ر is the لَامِ كَلِمَةٌ. Once, this is established, it is easy to compare any of its forms with the rest of table.

Below, we are providing a list of the basic forms (وَاحِدٌ مُذَكَّرٌ غَائِبٌ) of various verbs and their meanings. Their remaining forms can be created from them.

Word List For Verbs

English	Arabic
he wrote	كَتَبَ
he read	قَرَأَ
he found	وَجَدَ
he cooked	طَبَخَ
he cut	قَطَعَ
he filled	مَلَأَ
he sought, he demanded	طَلَبَ
he asked	سَأَلَ
he made	صَنَعَ
he took	أَخَذَ
he ate	أَكَلَ
he ran, he fled	هَرَبَ
he went	ذَهَبَ
he opened	فَتَحَ

اَلْفِعْلُ الْمَاضِي

English	Arabic
he hit	ضَرَبَ
he entered	دَخَلَ
he put (something)	وَضَعَ
he helped	نَصَرَ
he joined, he arrived	وَصَلَ
he returned	رَجَعَ
he slaughtered	ذَبَحَ
he oppressed	ظَلَمَ
he imprisoned, he detained	حَبَسَ

Exercise 1:   Translate into Arabic.
1. I wrote.
2. They (P/F) read.
3. You (S/M) found.
4. You (P/F) cooked.
5. They (P/F) cut.
6. We filled.
7. You (P/M) demanded.
8. They (D/M) asked.
9. They (D/F) made.
10. You (S/F) took.

Exercise 2:   Translate into Arabic.
1. It (S/M) was eaten.
2. They (P/M) were cut.
3. They (P/F) were made.
4. They (P/F) ran.
5. You (S/M) went.
6. You (P/M) were found.
7. It (S/F) was opened.
8. He was hit.
9. They (P/F) entered.
10. It (S/F) was placed.

Lesson 3

<u>Exercise 2:</u>   Translate into English and identify the *seeghah*.

1. نَصَرُوْا
2. فَتَحَتْ
3. ضَرَبْتُمْ
4. دَخَلْتُ
5. وَضَعَ
6. صَنَعْتِ
7. ذَهَبْنَا
8. وَجَدْتُنَّ
9. ذَهَبْتُمَا
10. كَتَبْنَا
11. قَرَأَتْ
12. طَبَخَا
13. أَكَلْنَ
14. وَصَلْتَ
15. هَرَبُوْا
16. رَجَعْتُمْ

<u>Exercise 3:</u>   Translate into English and identify the *seeghah*.

1. ضُرِبُوْا
2. نُصِرْتُ
3. ذُبِحَتْ
4. ظُلِمَتْ
5. قُطِعَ
6. وُضِعَتْ
7. صُنِعُوْا
8. خُلِقْتُمْ
9. خُلِقْنَا
10. حُبِسْتُمَا
11. وُجِدَنَا
12. سُئِلْتُنَّ

LESSON 4

فِعْلٌ، فَاعِلٌ، مَفْعُولٌ
Verb, Subject, Object

In Arabic, the word sequence in a verbal sentence is as follows: verb (فِعْلٌ), then subject (فَاعِلٌ), and finally the object (مَفْعُولٌ).

فِعْلٌ (verb) = the action being done.

فَاعِلٌ (subject) = the person doing the action.

مَفْعُولٌ (object) = the person or the thing to whom or to which the action is being done.

Rule: The فَاعِلٌ gets a *dammah* (or two *dammahs* as the case may be), and the مَفْعُولٌ gets a *fathah* (or two *fathahs*).

Examples:

1. 'Haamid helped Mahmood.' In this sentence, the فِعْلٌ is 'helped,' Haamid is the فَاعِلٌ and Mahmood is the مَفْعُولٌ. When translating this sentence into Arabic, the Arabic word for helped (نَصَرَ) will come first followed by the *faa'il*, Hamid (حَامِدٌ) with two *dammahs*, and then the *maf'ool*, Mahmood (مَحْمُودًا) with two *fathahs*. The final sentence will be نَصَرَ حَامِدٌ مَحْمُودًا.

2. 'A servant (خَادِمٌ) opened (فَتَحَ) a door (بَابًا).' The same order used for the last example (فِعْلٌ first, فَاعِلٌ second and مَفْعُولٌ last) will apply here. Remember, the فَاعِلٌ will get two *dammahs* and the مَفْعُولٌ will get two *fathahs*. The full sentence will be فَتَحَ خَادِمٌ بَابًا.

Notes:

- If there is an *alif-laam* on any word, the *tanween* (double *harakah*) at the end will change to a single *harakah* (the two *fathahs* will change to a single *fathah*, the two *kasrahs* will change to a single *kasrah*, and the two *dammahs* will change to a single *dammah*). Thus, 'the servant opened the door' will be written as فَتَحَ الْخَادِمُ الْبَابَ. Here, the *alif-laam* caused the double *harakah* to be dropped, and only a single *harakah* remained.

Lesson 4

- *Mudaaf* and *mudaaf ilayhi* can combine to form a فَاعِلٌ or a مَفْعُولٌ. For example:

  فَتَحَ خَادِمُ مَحْمُودٍ الْبَابَ

  Mahmood's servant opened the door.

  فَتَحَ الْخَادِمُ بَابَ الْبَيْتِ

  The servant opened the door of the house.

  فَتَحَ خَادِمُ مَحْمُودٍ بَابَ الْبَيْتِ

  Mahmood's servant opened the door of the house.

  In this case, it is important to remember that the *mudaaf* does not accept an *alif-laam* or a *tanween*. However, the *mudaaf ilayhi* can accept both. Moreover, the effect of being a فَاعِلٌ or مَفْعُولٌ will show on the *mudaaf* alone and not the *mudaaf ilayhi*.

Word List for Verbs

English	Arabic
he read	قَرَأَ
he stopped (someone)	مَنَعَ
he wrote	كَتَبَ
he defeated	هَزَمَ
he cooked	طَبَخَ
he ate	أَكَلَ
he hit; he beat	ضَرَبَ
he worshipped	عَبَدَ
he broke (something physical)	كَسَرَ
he tore	خَرَقَ
he helped	نَصَرَ
he cheated, he deceived	خَدَعَ
he profited	رَبِحَ
he heard	سَمِعَ
he made (someone into someone or something into something)	جَعَلَ

<u>فِعْلٌ، فَاعِلٌ، مَفْعُولٌ</u>

English	Arabic
he understood	فَهِمَ
he remembered	ذَكَرَ
he looked (at/towards)	نَظَرَ (إِلَى)
he broke (something non-physical)	نَقَضَ
he gave an example	ضَرَبَ (مَثَلًا)
he separated	فَرَقَ
he created, he made; he originated	خَلَقَ
he was ungrateful; disbelieved	كَفَرَ
he killed	قَتَلَ
he sat (down)	جَلَسَ
he imposed; he made something obligatory	كَتَبَ (عَلَى)

Word List for Nouns & Particles

English	Arabic	
	Singular	Plural
book	كِتَابٌ	كُتُبٌ
letter	رِسَالَةٌ	رَسَائِلُ
army	جُنْدٌ	جُنُودٌ
girl	بِنْتٌ	
meat	لَحْمٌ	لُحُومٌ
uncle (paternal)	عَمٌّ	
bread	خُبْزٌ	أَخْبَازٌ
rice	أُرْزٌ	
dog	كَلْبٌ	كِلَابٌ
(drinking) glass	كَأْسٌ	كُؤُوسٌ
garment, dress; cloth	ثَوْبٌ	ثِيَابٌ
friend	صَدِيقٌ	أَصْدِقَاءُ

Lesson 4

English	Arabic	
	Singular	Plural
mother	أُمٌّ	أُمَّهَاتٌ
messenger; prophet	رَسُوْلٌ	رُسُلٌ
religion	دِيْنٌ	أَدْيَانٌ
sky	سَمَاءٌ	سَمٰوٰتٌ (سَمٰوَاتٌ، سَمَاوَاتٌ)
building; roof	بِنَاءٌ	أَبْنِيَةٌ
land, earth	أَرْضٌ	أَرَاضٍ، اَلْأَرَاضِى
bed; spread; mattress	فِرَاشٌ	أَفْرِشَةٌ
Satan, the Devil	اَلشَّيْطَانُ	
not	مَا	
trade	تِجَارَةٌ	
ear	أُذْنٌ	أَذَانٌ
heart	قَلْبٌ	قُلُوْبٌ
transgressor	فَاسِقٌ	فَاسِقُوْنَ، فُسَّاقٌ
oath; pledge; promise	عَهْدٌ	عُهُوْدٌ
Muslim	مُسْلِمٌ	مُسْلِمُوْنَ
speech	كَلَامٌ	
man	رَجُلٌ	
example	مَثَلٌ	أَمْثَالٌ
blessing	نِعْمَةٌ	نِعَمٌ
sea	بَحْرٌ	بِحَارٌ
chicken, hen	دَجَاجَةٌ	دُجَجٌ
servant	خَادِمٌ	خُدَّامٌ
door	بَابٌ	أَبْوَابٌ

Exercise 1:   Translate into Arabic

1. Hameed read a book.
2. Naseer stopped Mahmood.
3. Khalid wrote a letter.

فِعْلٌ، فَاعِلٌ، مَفْعُولٌ

4. Tariq defeated the army.
5. The girl cooked the meat.
6. The uncle (maternal) ate the bread.
7. I ate the rice.
8. I hit the dog.
9. You (P/M) worshipped Allah.
10. You (S/F) tore the cloth.
11. Hameed's friend helped Khalid's grandson (son's son).
12. The girl's mother broke the glass.

Exercise 2: Translate into English and identify the فِعْلٌ, فَاعِلٌ, and مَفْعُولٌ, where applicable.

1. جَعَلَ اللهُ مُحَمَّدًا (صَلَّى اللهُ عَلَيْهِ وَ سَلَّمَ) رَسُولًا
2. جَعَلَ اللهُ الْإِسْلَامَ دِينًا
3. جَعَلَ اللهُ السَّمَاءَ بِنَاءً وَالْأَرْضَ فِرَاشًا
4. خَدَعَ الشَّيْطَانُ الْإِنْسَانَ
5. مَا رَبِحَتِ التِّجَارَةُ
6. سَمِعَتِ الْأُذَانَ وَعَقَلَتِ الْقُلُوبُ
7. نَقَضَ الْفَاسِقُ عَهْدَ اللهِ وَ سَمِعَ الْمُسْلِمُ كَلَامَ اللهِ
8. ضَرَبَ رَجُلٌ مَثَلًا
9. ذَكَرُوا نِعْمَةَ اللهِ وَمَا كَفَرُوا
10. فَرَقْنَا الْبَحْرَ
11. ذَبَحْتُمُ الدَّجَاجَةَ وَطَبَخْتُمُ اللَّحْمَ

LESSON 5

اَلْحُرُوفُ الْجَارَّةُ
Prepositions

The following particles are used as prepositions in Arabic. They occur quite frequently.

Table 5.1
Prepositions (اَلْحُرُوفُ الْجَارَّةُ)

in; regarding	فِي	with; at	بِ
from; than	مِنْ	to; up to	إِلَى
on; upon	عَلَى	for; belongs to	لِ
as, like	كَ	up to, until	حَتَّى
about; from; regarding	عَنْ	by (for oath)	وَ

The words that come after these prepositions end with a *kasrah* on the final letter. Below, we give examples of each of these.

زَيْدٌ فِي الدَّارِ	=	Zayd is in the house.
كَتَبْتُ بِالْقَلَمِ	=	I wrote with the pen.
مِنَ الْبَيْتِ إِلَى الْمَسْجِدِ	=	from the house to the mosque
جَلَسَ زَيْدٌ عَلَى الْكُرْسِيِّ	=	Zayd sat on the chair.
اَلسَّيَّارَةُ لِزَيْدٍ	=	The car belongs to Zayd.
أَحْمَدُ كَأَسَدٍ	=	Ahmad is like a lion.
نِمْتُ حَتَّى الصُّبْحِ	=	I slept until the morning.
سَأَلَتْ عَنِ الْكِتَابِ	=	She asked about the book.
وَاللهِ	=	By Allah!

Besides the ten prepositions listed above, there are seven other prepositions that occur less frequently. Since they do occur; therefore, it is appropriate to mention them as well. They are as follows:

1. تَ: by (for oath). This is specific with Allah, the Exalted. Example: تَاللهِ – By Allah!

25

Lesson 5

2 & 3. مُنْذُ وَ مُذْ: since. These are used to define a time period. Example: مَا ذَهَبْتُ إِلَى الْمَدْرَسَةِ مُنْذُ يَوْمِ الْجُمُعَةِ – I have not gone to the school since Friday.

4. رُبَّ: many a, so many. The noun used after رُبَّ is always singular. Example: رُبَّ رَجُلٍ نَصَرْتُهُ – I helped so many men.

5. خَلَا: besides, except. Example: عَلَّمْتُ الْأَطْفَالَ خَلَا زَيْدٍ – I taught the children except Zayd.

6. حَاشَا: besides, except. Example: مَنَعْتُ الرِّجَالَ حَاشَا عَمْرٍو – I stopped the men except 'Amr.

7. عَدَا: besides, except. Example: جَاءَ الْقَوْمُ عَدَا خَالِدٍ – The people came except Khalid.

Word List for Verbs

English	Arabic
he went	ذَهَبَ
he killed	قَتَلَ
he cut	قَطَعَ
he milked	حَلَبَ
he wrote	كَتَبَ
he ate	أَكَلَ
he asked	سَأَلَ
he made	جَعَلَ
he looked (at)	نَظَرَ (إِلَى)
he opened	فَتَحَ
he sat	جَلَسَ
he read	قَرَأَ
it (M) fell	وَقَعَ
it (M) was prescribed (upon)	كُتِبَ (عَلَى)
he broke	كَسَرَ

Word List for Nouns

English	Arabic Singular	Arabic Plural
village	قَرْيَةٌ	قُرًى
city	مَدِينَةٌ	مُدُنٌ
lion	أَسَدٌ	أُسْدٌ
sword	سَيْفٌ	سُيُوفٌ
cloth; clothes	ثَوْبٌ	ثِيَابٌ
scissors	مِقْرَاضٌ	مَقَارِيضُ
cow	بَقَرَةٌ	
milk	لَبَنٌ	أَلْبَانٌ
large bowl	قَصْعَةٌ	قِصَعٌ، قَصَعَاتٌ
card	بِطَاقَةٌ	بِطَاقَاتٌ
pencil	مِرْسَمٌ	مَرَاسِمُ
biscuit	كَعْكَةٌ	كَعْكٌ
butter	زُبْدَةٌ	
cream	قِشْطَةٌ	
teacher	أُسْتَاذٌ	أَسَاتِذَةُ
student	تِلْمِيذٌ	تَلَامِيذُ، تَلَامِذَةٌ
lesson	دَرْسٌ	دُرُوسٌ
night-time	لَيْلٌ	
sleep; sleeping	نَوْمٌ	
day-time	نَهَارٌ	أَنْهُرٌ
buffalo	جَامُوسٌ	جَوَامِيسُ
white; whiter	أَبْيَضُ	
gold	ذَهَبٌ	
silver	فِضَّةٌ	
stone	حَجَرٌ	أَحْجَارٌ، حِجَارَةٌ
moon	قَمَرٌ	أَقْمَارٌ

Lesson 5

English	Arabic Singular	Arabic Plural
star	نَجْمٌ	نُجُومٌ
lock	قُفْلٌ	أَقْفَالٌ
key	مِفْتَاحٌ	مَفَاتِيْحُ
garden	بُسْتَانٌ	بَسَاتِيْنُ
grass	عُشْبٌ	أَعْشَابٌ
praise	حَمْدٌ	
right guidance	هُدًى	
people		نَاسٌ
clouds (collective noun)	سَحَابٌ	
something which is under control	مُسَخَّرٌ	
between; among, amidst	بَيْنَ	
sky	سَمَاءٌ	سَمٰوٰتٌ (سَمٰوَاتٌ، سَمَاوَاتٌ)
land, earth	أَرْضٌ	أَرَاضٍ، ٱلْأَرَاضِي
Friday	يَوْمُ الْجُمُعَةِ	
Saturday	يَوْمُ السَّبْتِ	
Sunday	يَوْمُ الْأَحَدِ	
Monday	يَوْمُ الْاِثْنَيْنِ	
Tuesday	يَوْمُ الثَّلَاثَاءِ	
Wednesday	يَوْمُ الْأَرْبَعَاءِ يَوْمُ الْأَرْبَعَاءِ	
Thursday	يَوْمُ الْخَمِيْسِ	
Jew; Jewish	يَهُوْدِيٌّ	اَلْيَهُوْدُ
Christian	نَصْرَانِيٌّ	نَصَارَى
part, portion	جُزْءٌ	أَجْزَاءٌ
good deed	حَسَنَةٌ	حَسَنَاتٌ
world	دُنْيَا	
hereafter	آخِرَةٌ	

English	Arabic	
	Singular	Plural
fly	ذُبَابٌ	أَذِبَّةٌ
food	طَعَامٌ	
ritual prayer (*salah*)	صَلَاةٌ، صَلوةٌ	
door	بَابٌ	أَبْوَابٌ
room	حُجْرَةٌ	حُجُرَاتٌ
	غُرْفَةٌ	غُرَفٌ
bed	سَرِيرٌ	أَسِرَّةٌ
today	اَلْيَوْمَ	
tomorrow	غَدًا	
yesterday	أَمْسِ	

Exercise 1:   Translate into Arabic

1. Zayd went from the village to the city.
2. Mahmood killed the lion with the sword.
3. I cut the cloth with the scissors.
4. She milked the cow's milk in the bowl.
5. You (S/M) put the shirt and the pants (one pair) in the box.
6. You (P/M) wrote on the cards with pencils.
7. They (P/F) ate biscuits with butter and cream.
8. By Allah (oath).
9. The teacher asked the students about the lesson.
10. Allah made the night-time for sleeping and the day-time for working.
11. Buffalo's milk is whiter than cow's milk.
12. Gold and silver are like stones to Zahid.
13. I looked towards the moon and the stars.
14. They (P/M) opened the lock with the key.
15. We went to the garden and we sat on the grass.

Exercise 2:   Translate into English

1. اَلْحَمْدُ لِلَّهِ
2. فِى الْقُرْآنِ هُدًى لِلنَّاسِ
3. اَلسَّحَابُ مُسَخَّرٌ بَيْنَ السَّمَاءِ وَالْأَرْضِ

Lesson 5

4. يَوْمُ السَّبْتِ لِلْيَهُودِ وَيَوْمُ الأَحَدِ لِلنَّصَارَى
5. قَرَأْتُ جُزْءًا مِنَ الْقُرْآنِ فِي يَوْمِ الْخَمِيسِ وَالْجُمُعَةِ
6. لِلْمُسْلِمِ فِي الدُّنْيَا حَسَنَةٌ وَفِي الْآخِرَةِ حَسَنَةٌ
7. وَقَعَ الذُّبَابُ فِي الطَّعَامِ
8. كُتِبَتِ الصَّلَوةُ عَلَى الْمُسْلِمِ
9. فَتَحُوا بَابَ الْحُجْرَةِ يَوْمَ الاثْنَيْنِ وَجَلَسُوا عَلَى السَّرِيرِ يَوْمَ الثَّلَاثَاءِ

LESSON 6

اَلضَّمَائِرُ
Pronouns

A pronoun is called ضَمِيرٌ in Arabic. Its plural is ضَمَائِرُ. There are a number of different types of pronouns in Arabic. We are listing below those pronouns that are unattached (مُنْفَصِلٌ). These *dameers* are not joined to any word but appear as separate words. They can appear as *mubtada*. These should be memorized.

Table 6.1
Unattached (مُنْفَصِلٌ) Pronouns

Person	Gender	Plurality	Pronouns	
			English	Arabic
Third Person (غَائِبٌ)	Masculine (مُذَكَّرٌ)	Singular	he	هُوَ
		Dual	they	هُمَا
		Plural	they	هُمْ
	Feminine (مُؤَنَّثٌ)	Singular	she	هِيَ
		Dual	they	هُمَا
		Plural	they	هُنَّ
Second Person (حَاضِرٌ)	Masculine (مُذَكَّرٌ)	Singular	you	أَنْتَ
		Dual	you	أَنْتُمَا
		Plural	you	أَنْتُمْ
	Feminine (مُؤَنَّثٌ)	Singular	you	أَنْتِ
		Dual	you	أَنْتُمَا
		Plural	you	أَنْتُنَّ
First Person (مُتَكَلِّمٌ)	Masculine/Feminine	Singular	I	أَنَا
	Masculine/Feminine	Dual/Plural	we	نَحْنُ

Lesson 6

Below, we list the attached (مُتَّصِلٌ) *dameers*. They are also called possessive (إِضَافِيٌّ) and objective (مَفْعُولِيٌّ) *dameers*. By possessive, we mean those pronouns, which indicate possession (إِضَافَةٌ); and by objective we mean those pronouns, which refer to the object (مَفْعُولٌ).

Table 6.2
Attached (مُتَّصِلٌ) Pronouns

Person	Gender	Plurality	Pronouns English	Arabic
Third Person (غَائِبٌ)	Masculine (مُذَكَّرٌ)	Singular	his, him	هُ
		Dual	their, them	هُمَا
		Plural	their, them	هُمْ
	Feminine (مُؤَنَّثٌ)	Singular	hers, her	هَا
		Dual	their, them	هُمَا
		Plural	their, them	هُنَّ
Second Person (حَاضِرٌ)	Masculine (مُذَكَّرٌ)	Singular	your, you	كَ
		Dual	your, you	كُمَا
		Plural	your, you	كُمْ
	Feminine (مُؤَنَّثٌ)	Singular	your, you	كِ
		Dual	your, you	كُمَا
		Plural	your, you	كُنَّ
First Person (مُتَكَلِّمٌ)	Masculine/Feminine	Singular	my, me	يْ ، نِيْ
	Masculine/Feminine	Dual/Plural	ours, us	نَا

Examples of Usage of Unattached *Dameers*

هُوَ زَيْدٌ	–	He is Zayd.
أَنَا طَالِبٌ	–	I am a student.
أَنْتَ مُجْتَهِدٌ	–	You are hardworking.

Examples of Usage of Attached *Dameers*

These pronouns can come after nouns, verbs and particles as shown in the examples below.

1. After a noun, showing attribution/possession (إِضَافَةٌ):

    قَلَمُهُ – his (S/M) pen

    كِتَابُكَ – your (S/M) book

    كِتَابِي – my book

    كِتَابُهَا – her (S/F) book.

2. After a verb, indicating the object (مَفْعُوْلٌ):

    نَصَرْتُهُ – I helped him

    أَمَرْتُكَ – I commanded you

    نَصَرْتَنِي – you (S/M) helped me.

3. After a particle:

    فِيْهِ – in it

    لَهُ – for him

    مِنْكَ – from you (S/M)

    إِلَيْنَا – to/towards us

    إِنَّكُمْ – indeed you (P/M)

    عَلَيْهِ – on him.

Word List for Verbs

English	Arabic
he rode	رَكِبَ
he broke	كَسَرَ
he fell	سَقَطَ
he stopped (someone)	مَنَعَ

Lesson 6

English	Arabic
he raised (someone or something)	رَفَعَ
he played	لَعِبَ
he looked	نَظَرَ (إلى)
he worshipped	عَبَدَ
he remembered	ذَكَرَ
he ate	أَكَلَ
he provided livelihood/sustenance	رَزَقَ
he sealed, he put a seal	خَتَمَ
he cheated, he deceived	خَدَعَ
he left; he abandoned	تَرَكَ
he snatched	خَطَفَ
he created	خَلَقَ
he presented	عَرَضَ
he took	أَخَذَ
he did (good deeds); he acted (righteously)	عَمِلَ (صَالِحًا)

Word List for Nouns & Particles

English	Arabic Singular	Arabic Plural
father	أَبٌ	آبَاءٌ
mother	أُمٌّ	أُمَّهَاتٌ
tongue	لِسَانٌ	أَلْسِنَةٌ
head	رَأْسٌ	رُؤُوسٌ
nose	أَنْفٌ	أُنُوفٌ
hand	يَدٌ	أَيْدٍ، الأَيْدِي
tooth	سِنٌّ (سِنٌّ)	أَسْنَانٌ
chest	صَدْرٌ	صُدُورٌ

اَلضَّمَائِرُ

English	Arabic	
	Singular	Plural
handkerchief	مِنْدِيْلٌ	مَنَادِيْلُ
car	سَيَّارَةٌ	سَيَّارَاتٌ
bicycle	دَرَّاجَةٌ	دَرَّاجَاتٌ
shoe	حِذَاءٌ	أَحْذِيَةٌ
foot	رِجْلٌ ، قَدَمٌ	
ball	كُرَةٌ	كُرَاتٌ
mango	أَنْبَجْ، مَنْجُوْ	
apple	تُفَاحَةٌ	تُفَاحٌ
garden	بُسْتَانٌ	
melon, watermelon	بِطِّيْخٌ	
cucumber	قِثَّاءٌ	
field; arable land	حَقْلٌ	حُقُوْلٌ
heart	قَلْبٌ	قُلُوْبٌ
hearing; also used for ears	سَمْعٌ	
eyesight; glance; also used for eyes	بَصَرٌ	أَبْصَارٌ
veil, covering	غِشَاوَةٌ	
themselves	أَنْفُسُهُمْ	
darkness	ظُلْمَةٌ	ظُلُمَاتٌ (ظُلْمَتٌ)
lightning	بَرْقٌ	
Lord	رَبٌّ	
fuel	وَقُوْدٌ	
people		نَاسٌ
stone	حَجَرٌ	حِجَارَةٌ
husband; wife; spouse	زَوْجٌ	أَزْوَاجٌ
clean, pure (F)	مُطَهَّرَةٌ	
angel	مَلَكٌ	مَلَائِكَةٌ

Lesson 6

English	Arabic	
	Singular	Plural
covenant	مِيْثَاقٌ	مَوَائِيْقُ
above	فَوْقَ	
Mount Sinai	طُوْرٌ	
color	لَوْنٌ	أَلْوَانٌ
bright yellow	فَاقِعٌ	
whoever	مَنْ	
then; so; therefore; sometimes, it is not translated	فَ	
compensation, reward	أَجْرٌ	أُجُوْرٌ
with	عِنْدَ	

Exercise 1: Translate into Arabic

1. My father
2. His mother
3. Her tongue
4. Your (S/M) head
5. Your (S/F) nose
6. My hand
7. Their (P/F) teeth
8. His chest
9. Our handkerchief
10. I rode in your (S/M) car.
11. She broke my bike.
12. The shoe fell off your (S/M) foot.
13. I stopped them (P/F).
14. They (P/M) raised me.
15. You (P/M) played with the ball.
16. They (D/M) looked at me.
17. You (D/F) worshipped Him.
18. My mother remembered me yesterday.
19. You (S/M) ate a mango and an apple in your garden and you ate a watermelon and a cucumber in your field.

اَلضَّمَائِرُ

Exercise 2:   Translate into English

1. رَزَقْنَاهُمْ
2. خَتَمَ اللهُ عَلَى قُلُوبِهِمْ وَعَلَى سَمْعِهِمْ
3. عَلَى أَبْصَارِهِمْ غِشَاوَةٌ
4. خَدَعُوا أَنْفُسَهُمْ
5. تَرَكَهُمْ فِي ظُلُمَٰتٍ
6. خَطَفَ البَرْقُ أَبْصَارَهُمْ
7. إِنَّ رَبَّكُمْ خَلَقَكُمْ
8. وَقُودُهَا النَّاسُ وَالحِجَارَةُ
9. لَهُمْ فِيهَا أَزْوَاجٌ مُطَهَّرَةٌ
10. عَرَضَهُمْ عَلَى المَلَٰئِكَةِ
11. أَخَذْنَا مِيثَاقَكُمْ وَرَفَعْنَا فَوْقَكُمُ الطُّورَ
12. لَوْنُهَا فَاقِعٌ
13. مَنْ عَمِلَ صَالِحًا فَلَهُ أَجْرُهُ

LESSON 7

اَلْفِعْلُ الْمُضَارِعُ
Present and Future Tense Verb

We have already discussed the past tense verb and pronouns. In this lesson, we will discuss فِعْلٌ مُضَارِعٌ which is equivalent to present and future tense. فِعْلٌ مَاضٍ (past tense) and فِعْلٌ مُضَارِعٌ (present/future tense), as well as ضَمَائِرُ (pronouns) are the foundations of the Arabic language. These should be memorized properly. This will make all future lessons much easier. We are listing below the conjugations (verb forms) of فِعْلٌ مُضَارِعٌ (present and future tense verb) in active voice (مَعْرُوْفٌ).

Table 7.1
Verb Forms of (فِعْلٌ مُضَارِعٌ) in Active Voice (مَعْرُوْفٌ)

Person	Gender	Plurality	English	Arabic
Third Person (غَائِبٌ)	Masculine (مُذَكَّرٌ)	Singular	He/It is doing or will do	يَفْعَلُ
		Dual	They are doing or will do	يَفْعَلَانِ
		Plural	They are doing or will do	يَفْعَلُوْنَ
	Feminine (مُؤَنَّثٌ)	Singular	She/It is doing or will do	تَفْعَلُ
		Dual	They are doing or will do	تَفْعَلَانِ
		Plural	They are doing or will do	يَفْعَلْنَ
Second Person (حَاضِرٌ)	Masculine (مُذَكَّرٌ)	Singular	You are doing or will do	تَفْعَلُ
		Dual	You are doing or will do	تَفْعَلَانِ
		Plural	You are doing or will do	تَفْعَلُوْنَ

Lesson 7

Table 7.1 *Continued*

Second Person (حَاضِرٌ)	Feminine (مُؤَنَّثٌ)	Singular	You are doing or will do	تَفْعَلِينَ
		Dual	You are doing or will do	تَفْعَلَانِ
		Plural	You are doing or will do	تَفْعَلْنَ
First Person (مُتَكَلِّمٌ)	Masculine/Feminine	Singular	I am doing or will do	أَفْعَلُ
	Masculine/Feminine	Dual/Plural	We are doing or will do	نَفْعَلُ

Before we move on, it would be useful to see how Table 7.1 would be written in Arabic. This is as follows:

Table 7.1a

اَلْفِعْلُ الْمُضَارِعُ الْمَعْرُوفُ

اَلصِّيْغَةُ	اِسْمُ الصِّيْغَةِ
يَفْعَلُ	وَاحِدٌ مُذَكَّرٌ غَائِبٌ
يَفْعَلَانِ	تَثْنِيَةٌ مُذَكَّرٌ غَائِبٌ
يَفْعَلُونَ	جَمْعٌ مُذَكَّرٌ غَائِبٌ
تَفْعَلُ	وَاحِدٌ مُؤَنَّثٌ غَائِبٌ
تَفْعَلَانِ	تَثْنِيَةٌ مُؤَنَّثٌ غَائِبٌ
يَفْعَلْنَ	جَمْعٌ مُؤَنَّثٌ غَائِبٌ
تَفْعَلُ	وَاحِدٌ مُذَكَّرٌ حَاضِرٌ
تَفْعَلَانِ	تَثْنِيَةٌ مُذَكَّرٌ حَاضِرٌ
تَفْعَلُونَ	جَمْعٌ مُذَكَّرٌ حَاضِرٌ
تَفْعَلِينَ	وَاحِدٌ مُؤَنَّثٌ حَاضِرٌ
تَفْعَلَانِ	تَثْنِيَةٌ مُؤَنَّثٌ حَاضِرٌ
تَفْعَلْنَ	جَمْعٌ مُؤَنَّثٌ حَاضِرٌ
أَفْعَلُ	وَاحِدٌ مُتَكَلِّمٌ
نَفْعَلُ	جَمْعٌ مُتَكَلِّمٌ

Creating Passive Voice فِعْلٌ مُضَارِعٌ

In lesson 3, we discussed the method of converting فِعْلٌ مَاضٍ مَعْرُوْفٌ (past tense active voice) to فِعْلٌ مَاضٍ مَجْهُوْلٌ (past tense passive voice). Now, we discuss the method of converting فِعْلٌ مُضَارِعٌ from active to passive voice. يَفْعَلُ, which means "he does or will do," is in active voice (مَعْرُوْفٌ). To convert this فِعْلٌ مُضَارِعٌ مَعْرُوْفٌ to فِعْلٌ مُضَارِعٌ مَجْهُوْلٌ, we give the first letter a *dammah* and the third letter a *fathah*. يَفْعَلُ becomes يُفْعَلُ, تَضْرِبُ becomes تُضْرَبُ, يَفْتَحُ becomes يُفْتَحُ, أَنْصُرُ becomes أُنْصَرُ, and so on.

Table 7.2
Verb Forms of (فِعْلٌ مُضَارِعٌ) in Passive Voice (مَجْهُوْلٌ)

Person	Gender	Plurality	English	Arabic
Third Person (غَائِبٌ)	Masculine (مُذَكَّرٌ)	Singular	He/It is being done or will be done	يُفْعَلُ
		Dual	They are being done or will be done	يُفْعَلَانِ
		Plural	They are being done or will be done	يُفْعَلُوْنَ
	Feminine (مُؤَنَّثٌ)	Singular	She/It is being done or will be done	تُفْعَلُ
		Dual	They are being done or will be done	تُفْعَلَانِ
		Plural	They are being done or will be done	يُفْعَلْنَ
Second Person (حَاضِرٌ)	Masculine (مُذَكَّرٌ)	Singular	You are being done or will be done	تُفْعَلُ
		Dual	You are being done or will be done	تُفْعَلَانِ
		Plural	You are being done or will be done	تُفْعَلُوْنَ
	Feminine (مُؤَنَّثٌ)	Singular	You are being done or will be done	تُفْعَلِيْنَ
		Dual	You are being done or will be done	تُفْعَلَانِ
		Plural	You are being done or will be done	تُفْعَلْنَ

Lesson 7

Table 7.2 *continued*

| First Person (مُتَكَلِّم) | Masculine/Feminine | Singular | I am being done or will be done | أُفْعَلُ |
| | Masculine/Feminine | Dual/Plural | We are being done or will be done | نُفْعَلُ |

Before we move on, it would be useful to see how Table 7.2 would be written in Arabic. This is as follows:

Table 7.2a
اَلْفِعْلُ الْمُضَارِعُ الْمَجْهُولُ

اَلصِّيغَةُ	اِسْمُ الصِّيغَةِ
يُفْعَلُ	وَاحِدٌ مُذَكَّرٌ غَائِبٌ
يُفْعَلَانِ	تَثْنِيَةٌ مُذَكَّرٌ غَائِبٌ
يُفْعَلُونَ	جَمْعٌ مُذَكَّرٌ غَائِبٌ
تُفْعَلُ	وَاحِدٌ مُؤَنَّثٌ غَائِبٌ
تُفْعَلَانِ	تَثْنِيَةٌ مُؤَنَّثٌ غَائِبٌ
يُفْعَلْنَ	جَمْعٌ مُؤَنَّثٌ غَائِبٌ
تُفْعَلُ	وَاحِدٌ مُذَكَّرٌ حَاضِرٌ
تُفْعَلَانِ	تَثْنِيَةٌ مُذَكَّرٌ حَاضِرٌ
تُفْعَلُونَ	جَمْعٌ مُذَكَّرٌ حَاضِرٌ
تُفْعَلِينَ	وَاحِدٌ مُؤَنَّثٌ حَاضِرٌ
تُفْعَلَانِ	تَثْنِيَةٌ مُؤَنَّثٌ حَاضِرٌ
تُفْعَلْنَ	جَمْعٌ مُؤَنَّثٌ حَاضِرٌ
أُفْعَلُ	وَاحِدٌ مُتَكَلِّمٌ
نُفْعَلُ	جَمْعٌ مُتَكَلِّمٌ

Note: When a passive verb is used, the فَاعِلٌ (subject) is not mentioned. Rather, the مَفْعُولٌ (object) takes the place of the فَاعِلٌ (subject) and is called نَائِبُ فَاعِلٍ (subject of the passive verb) or قَائِمٌ مَقَامَ فَاعِلٍ (substitute subject). Since it takes the place of the فَاعِلٌ, it also gets a *dammah*.

Examples:

ضُرِبَ الْوَلَدُ – The boy was hit.   فِعْلٌ مَاضٍ مَجْهُولٌ:

مُنِعَتِ الْمَرْأَةُ – The woman was stopped.

يُفْتَحُ الْبَابُ – The door will be opened.   فِعْلٌ مُضَارِعٌ مَجْهُولٌ:

يُكْسَرُ الْجِدَارُ – The wall will be broken.

Note: In the tables above, the first letter of each *seeghah* of مُضَارِعٌ, both مَعْرُوفٌ and مَجْهُولٌ, is called حَرْفُ الْمُضَارِعِ (plural: حُرُوفُ الْمُضَارِعِ). As can be seen in the table, these are ي, ت, أ, and ن.

Relationship between the *Seeghahs* of فِعْلٌ مَاضٍ and فِعْلٌ مُضَارِعٌ

Before we move on, it will be useful to keep in mind that the *'ayn kalimah* of the فِعْلٌ مَاضٍ and فِعْلٌ مُضَارِعٌ of a وَاحِدٌ مُذَكَّرٌ غَائِبٌ can vary in a number of different ways. It can have a *fathah*, *kasrah* or *dammah* in فِعْلٌ مَاضٍ and/or فِعْلٌ مُضَارِعٌ. It is beyond the scope of this book to discuss all of these combinations. However, at this stage, it is, nevertheless, important to take note of the *harakah* on the *'ayn kalimah* of any given فِعْلٌ مَاضٍ and its corresponding فِعْلٌ مُضَارِعٌ.

Word List for Verbs

English (for past tense)	Arabic	
	مَاضٍ	مُضَارِعٌ
he went	ذَهَبَ	يَذْهَبُ
he wandered about	عَمِهَ	يَعْمَهُ
he made (someone into someone or something into something)	جَعَلَ	يَجْعَلُ
he came to know	عَلِمَ	يَعْلَمُ

Lesson 7

English (for past tense)	Arabic	
	مَاضٍ	مُضَارِعٌ
he worshipped	عَبَدَ	يَعْبُدُ
he realized; he became aware	شَعَرَ	يَشْعُرُ
he heard	سَمِعَ	يَسْمَعُ
he played	لَعِبَ	يَلْعَبُ
he wore	لَبِسَ	يَلْبَسُ
he became sad, he grieved	حَزِنَ	يَحْزَنُ
he slaughtered	ذَبَحَ	يَذْبَحُ
he drank	شَرِبَ	يَشْرَبُ
he read	قَرَأَ	يَقْرَأُ
he cooked	طَبَخَ	يَطْبُخُ
he made (something)	صَنَعَ	يَصْنَعُ
he stopped (someone)	مَنَعَ	يَمْنَعُ
he opened	فَتَحَ	يَفْتَحُ
he washed	غَسَلَ	يَغْسِلُ
he laughed	ضَحِكَ	يَضْحَكُ
he was angry (with someone)	سَخِطَ (عَلَى فُلَانٍ)	يَسْخَطُ (عَلَى فُلَانٍ)
he broke (something non-physical); he nullified	نَقَضَ	يَنْقُضُ
he commanded, he ordered	أَمَرَ	يَأْمُرُ
he concealed	كَتَمَ	يَكْتُمُ
he wrote	كَتَبَ	يَكْتُبُ
he cut	قَطَعَ	يَقْطَعُ
he helped	نَصَرَ	يَنْصُرُ
he deceived, he cheated	خَدَعَ	يَخْدَعُ
he colored, he dyed	صَبَغَ	يَصْبَغُ
he raised	رَفَعَ	يَرْفَعُ
he sent	بَعَثَ	يَبْعَثُ

اَلْفِعْلُ الْمُضَارِعُ

English (for past tense)	Arabic	
	مَاضٍ	مُضَارِعٌ
he ate	أَكَلَ	يَأْكُلُ
he remembered; he mentioned	ذَكَرَ	يَذْكُرُ

Word List for Nouns & Particles

English	Arabic	
	Singular	Plural
food	طَعَامٌ	
newspaper	جَرِيدَةٌ	جَرَائِدُ
potato	بَطَاطَا	
tea	شَايٌ	
spoon	مِلْعَقَةٌ	مَلَاعِقُ
lock	قُفْلٌ	
key	مِفْتَاحٌ	
washerman	قَصَّارٌ	
cloth; clothes	ثَوْبٌ	ثِيَابٌ
pond, pool	غَدِيرٌ	غُدُرٌ
laughter	ضَحْكٌ، ضِحْكٌ	
friend	صَدِيقٌ	
house	بَيْتٌ	
prayer leader; leader	إِمَامٌ	أَئِمَّةٌ
people		نَاسٌ
what?; do...?; will...?; etc. (depending on the context)	أَ ، هَلْ	
sinfulness	فِسْقٌ	
disbelief, infidelity	كُفْرٌ	
today	اَلْيَوْمَ	
tommorrow	غَدًا	

Lesson 7

English	Arabic	
	Singular	Plural
day after tomorrow	بَعْدَ غَدٍ	
a year ago	قَبْلَ سَنَةٍ	
day before yesterday	قَبْلَ الْأَمْسِ	
letter	رِسَالَةٌ	
paternal uncle	عَمٌّ	
fear	خَوْفٌ	
promise; pledge	عَهْدٌ	
that, which	مَا	
piety, righteousness	بِرٌّ	
that; to	أَنْ	
cow	بَقَرَةٌ	
speech	كَلَامٌ	
rope	حَبْلٌ	جِبَالٌ
remembrance	ذِكْرٌ	
prophet	رَسُولٌ ، نَبِيٌّ	
fruit	فَاكِهَةٌ	فَوَاكِهُ
library	مَكْتَبَةٌ، خَزَانَةُ الْكُتُبِ	مَكْتَبَاتٌ، مَكَاتِبُ
magazine	مَجَلَّةٌ	مَجَلَّاتٌ
article; essay	مَقَالَةٌ	مَقَالَاتٌ

Exercise 1:   Translate into English

1. أَذْهَبُ
2. يَعْمَهُونَ
3. يَجْعَلُ
4. أَعْلَمُ
5. نَعْبُدُ
6. تَشْعُرُونَ
7. تَسْمَعِينَ
8. تَلْعَبِينَ
9. يَلْبَسْنَ
10. تَخْزَنَانِ
11. يَذْبَحَانِ
12. أَشْرَبُ

اَلْفِعْلُ الْمُضَارِعُ

Exercise 2:   Translate into Arabic

1. They (P/M) came to know.
2. You (P/F) are reading.
3. She is cooking.
4. He is grieving.
5. They (P/F) are cooking.
6. I am making food.
7. We will drink.
8. You (S/F) will go.
9. You (S/M) will stop.
10. They (D/M) will go.

Exercise 3:   Translate into Arabic

1. I will read your (S/M) newspaper.
2. They (P/F) will cook a potato for you (P/M).
3. You (P/M) are drinking tea with a spoon.
4. Your (P/M) uncle (paternal) will open the lock with his key.
5. The washerman is washing the clothes in the pond.
6. Haamid is laughing in his house.
7. I am hearing his laughter in my house.
8. Khalid's friend will go to your (S/M) house.
9. We will make you (S/M) a leader for the people.
10. Are you (P/F) stopping them (P/M) from sinfulness and disbelief?
11. Today I read your (S/F) letter.
12. Tomorrow I will go to her uncle's (paternal) house.
13. Are you (S/F) angry with him?

Exercise 4:   Translate into English

1. لَا خَوْفٌ عَلَيْهِمْ وَلَا هُمْ يَحْزَنُونَ
2. يَنْقُضُونَ عَهْدَ اللهِ
3. إِنِّي أَعْلَمُ مَا لَا تَعْلَمُونَ
4. أَتَأْمُرُونَ النَّاسَ بِالْبِرِّ
5. نَحْنُ لَا نَكْتُمُ مَا أَمَرَنَا اللهُ
6. اللهُ يَأْمُرُكُمْ أَنْ تَذْبَحُوا بَقَرَةً
7. يَسْمَعُونَ كَلَامَ اللهِ

Lesson 7

Exercise 5: Translate into Arabic

1. Is being read (S/M, third person)
2. Is being written (S/M, third person)
3. Will be broken (S/M, third person)
4. Will be cut (S/M, third person)
5. She is being helped.
6. You are being stopped (S/M)
7. I am being stopped.
8. We are being helped.
9. You (S/F) will be stopped.
10. You (S/M) are being cheated.

Exercise 6: Translate into Arabic

1. The rope is being cut.
2. The cloth will be dyed.
3. Remembrance of the Prophet (Allah bless him and give him peace) is being raised.
4. The prophets are being sent.
5. Fruits are being eaten.
6. Allah is being remembered.
7. Tomorrow, the newspaper will be read in the library.
8. An article will be written for your (S/F) magazine the day after tomorrow.
9. The promise was broken a year ago.

LESSON 8

اَلصِّفَةُ وَ الْمَوْصُوْفُ
Adjective

Consider the following phrases: 'truthful Muslim,' 'pious man,' 'large mosque,' 'small book,' 'trustworthy servant.' These phrases and other phrases of similar pattern are called صِفَةٌ (adjective) and مَوْصُوْفٌ (the described). In the phrase 'small book,' 'small' describes the 'book.' Thus, 'small' is صِفَةٌ (adjective), and 'book' is مَوْصُوْفٌ (the described).

To convert such a phrase into Arabic, follow the following steps:
1. Translate the individual words into Arabic.
2. Reverse the order of the words so that the first word comes second and the second word comes first.
3. Give both words one or two *dammah(s)* (depending on the situation).

Example: We want to convert the phrase, 'truthful Muslim' into Arabic. First, we translate the individual words into Arabic. We get صَادِق مُسْلِم. Next, we reverse the order to get مُسْلِم صَادِق. Then, we give two *dammahs* to both the words. We get مُسْلِمٌ صَادِقٌ. Similarly, if we want to convert 'pious man' into Arabic, we will first translate the individual words into Arabic – صَالِح رَجُل. Next, we will reverse the order of the words – رَجُل صَالِح. Lastly, we will give two *dammahs* to both words – رَجُلٌ صَالِحٌ.

States of Nouns:

Before we move on, it will be useful to keep in mind that each noun is always in a certain state. There are three states in total for nouns. These are as follows:

1. رَفْعٌ: This is the state when a noun has one or two *dammahs* at the end. Such a noun is called مَرْفُوْعٌ. For example, بَيْتٌ or اَلْبَيْتُ.

2. نَصْبٌ: This is the state when a noun has one or two *fathahs* at the end. Such a noun is called مَنْصُوْبٌ. For example, بَيْتًا or اَلْبَيْتَ.

3. جَرٌّ: This is the state when a noun has one or two *kasrahs* at the end. Such a noun is called مَجْرُوْرٌ. For example, بَيْتٍ or اَلْبَيْتِ.

Note: There is another state which is specific to verbs. This is جَزْمٌ. This is the

Lesson 8

condition in which a سُكُوْنٌ appears at the end of a word or its substitute (ن in the case of فِعْلٌ مُضَارِعٌ) is dropped from the end. Such a word is said to be مَجْزُوْمٌ. For example, لَمْ يَضْرِبْ (he did not hit).

Additional Rules for صِفَةٌ **and** مَوْصُوْفٌ:

1. Both the صِفَةٌ and the مَوْصُوْفٌ have to be in the same state, i.e., if one is مَرْفُوْعٌ, then the other should also be مَرْفُوْعٌ. Similarly, if one is مَنْصُوْبٌ, the other should also be مَنْصُوْبٌ. For example, consider رَجُلٌ صَالِحٌ. Since رَجُلٌ has two *dammahs* at the end, it is مَرْفُوْعٌ; therefore, صَالِحٌ will also be given two *dammahs* to make it مَرْفُوْعٌ. Similarly, if for some reason رَجُلٌ was مَنْصُوْبٌ, صَالِحٌ would also have to be مَنْصُوْبٌ. The phrase would then have been رَجُلًا صَالِحًا such as in نَصَرْتُ رَجُلًا صَالِحًا (I helped a pious man). If رَجُلٌ had been مَجْرُوْرٌ, صَالِحٌ would also have been مَجْرُوْرٌ. The phrase would then have been رَجُلٍ صَالِحٍ such as in ذَهَبْتُ إِلَى رَجُلٍ صَالِحٍ (I went to a pious man).

2. Both the صِفَةٌ and the مَوْصُوْفٌ should either be *ma'rifah* or *nakirah*. Thus, if the مَوْصُوْفٌ has an *alif-laam*, the صِفَةٌ should also have an *alif-laam*. For example, if رَجُلٌ were to be changed to اَلرَّجُلُ, صَالِحٌ would also change to اَلصَّالِحُ.

3. The gender of the صِفَةٌ and the مَوْصُوْفٌ should be the same. Thus, if the مَوْصُوْفٌ is feminine, the صِفَةٌ should also be feminine. To change a word to its feminine form, just add a round *taa* (ة) at the end of the word. For example, 'a pious teacher (F)' will be أُسْتَاذَةٌ صَالِحَةٌ and 'the pious teacher (F)' will be اَلْأُسْتَاذَةُ الصَّالِحَةُ.

4. If the مَوْصُوْفٌ is a proper noun, it will not accept *alif-laam*. For non-proper nouns *alif-laam* is used to change *nakirah* into *ma'rifah*. However, all proper nouns are considered *ma'rifah* by default even without an *alif-laam*. Since, the مَوْصُوْفٌ is a proper noun; therefore, the صِفَةٌ will require an *alif-laam* to make it *ma'rifah*. For example, when converting 'the conqueror Khalid' into Arabic, we will not add *alif-laam* to خَالِدٌ because it is already a

proper noun. However, we will add an *alif-laam* to the صِفَة (فَاتِحٌ) because it is not a proper noun. The sentence will be خَالِدٌ الْفَاتِحُ.

The following examples illustrate this point:

'The king Mahmood' will be مَحْمُودٌ الْمَلِكُ.

'The commander Taariq' will be طَارِقٌ الْقَائِدُ.

'The poet Ghalib' will be غَالِبٌ الشَّاعِرُ.

These sentences can also be <u>read</u> (not written) as مَحْمُودٌ نِالْمَلِكُ, خَالِدٌ نِالْفَاتِحُ, غَالِبٌ نِالشَّاعِرُ and طَارِقٌ نِالْقَائِدُ.

Word List for Verbs

English	Arabic
he drank	شَرِبَ
he defeated	هَزَمَ
he entered	دَخَلَ
he touched, he felt (by hand); he examined	جَسَّ
he provided	رَزَقَ
he conquered	فَتَحَ
he took	أَخَذَ

Word List for Nouns

English	Arabic	
	Singular	Plural
pious, righteous	صَالِحٌ	
father	أَبٌ	
son	اِبْنٌ	
most-forgiving	غَفُورٌ	
Lord	رَبٌّ	
big, large	كَبِيرٌ	كِبَارٌ

Lesson 8

English	Arabic	
	Singular	Plural
door	بَابٌ	
old	قَدِيمٌ	
mat	حَصِيرٌ	حُصُرٌ
good; excellent	جَيِّدٌ	
article; essay	مَقَالَةٌ	
magazine	مَجَلَّةٌ	
street	شَارِعٌ	شَوَارِعُ
small, little	صَغِيرٌ	صِغَارٌ
ship, boat	سَفِينَةٌ	سُفُنٌ
deep	عَمِيقٌ	
sea	بَحْرٌ	بِحَارٌ
great; powerful	عَظِيمٌ	عُظَمَاءُ
mountain	جَبَلٌ	جِبَالٌ
long	طَوِيلٌ	
train	قِطَارٌ	قُطُرٌ
train engine	قَاطِرَةٌ	قَاطِرَاتٌ
station	مَحَطَّةٌ	مَحَطَّاتٌ
immoral person	فَاجِرٌ	فُجَّارٌ
	فَاسِقٌ	فُسَّاقٌ
man	رَجُلٌ	
beautiful, handsome; good	حَسَنٌ	حِسَانٌ
fan	مِرْوَحَةٌ	
sick, ill	مَرِيضٌ	مَرْضَى
woman	امْرَأَةٌ	
bitter	مُرٌّ	
medicine	دَوَاءٌ	أَدْوِيَةٌ
king	مَلِكٌ	مُلُوكٌ

اَلصِّفَةُ وَالْمَوْصُوفُ

English	Arabic Singular	Plural
army	جُنْدٌ	جُنُودٌ
capital city	عَاصِمَةٌ	عَوَاصِمُ
today	اَلْيَوْمَ	
skillful; outstanding	بَارِعٌ، مَاهِرٌ	
barber	حَلَّاقٌ	
store, shop	دُكَّانٌ	دَكَاكِينُ
old man; scholar	شَيْخٌ	شُيُوخٌ
mischievous	شِرِّيرٌ	أَشِرَّاءُ
boy	وَلَدٌ	
ugly	دَمِيمٌ	دِمَامٌ
near, close	قَرِيبٌ (مِنْ)	
house	بَيْتٌ	
doctor	طَبِيبٌ	أَطِبَّاءُ
medical prescription	وَصْفَةٌ	
path	صِرَاطٌ	
straight	مُسْتَقِيمٌ	
torment; punishment	عَذَابٌ	
painful	أَلِيمٌ	
mosquito	بَعُوضَةٌ	
livelihood	رِزْقٌ	أَرْزَاقٌ
trial, tribulation	بَلَاءٌ	
night	لَيْلَةٌ	لَيَالٍ (اَللَّيَالِي)
dark	مُظْلِمَةٌ	
example	مَثَلٌ	
word	كَلِمَةٌ	كَلِمَاتٌ
tree	شَجَرَةٌ	شَجَرَاتٌ
good; pleasant (F)	طَيِّبَةٌ	طَيِّبَاتٌ

Lesson 8

English	Arabic	
	Singular	Plural
root	أَصْلٌ	أُصُوْلٌ
firm, established	ثَابِتٌ	
branch	فَرْعٌ	فُرُوْعٌ
sky	سَمَاءٌ	
commander, leader	قَائِدٌ	
city	مَدِيْنَةٌ	
fort, fortress, castle	حِصْنٌ	حُصُوْنٌ
hand; possession	يَدٌ	
conqueror	فَاتِحٌ	
Romans	اَلرُّوْمُ	

Exercise 1: Translate into Arabic

1. Pious father
2. The son Sa'eed
3. Most-forgiving Lord
4. Big door
5. The old mat
6. Good article
7. Good magazine
8. Big street
9. Small boat
10. Deep sea
11. Great mountain
12. Long train
13. Big engine
14. Small station

Exercise 2: Translate into Arabic

1. I hit an immoral man.
2. You (P/M) took a beautiful fan.
3. The sick woman drank bitter medicine.
4. Brave Tariq defeated a big king's army and he entered his capital.
5. Today I will go to a skilled barber's shop.

6. This is a pious old man and that is a mischievous child.
7. This is a handsome man and that is an ugly boy.
8. You (S/M) went to a shop close to your house.
9. Doctor Mahmood examined a sick woman and wrote a good prescription for her.

<u>Exercise 3:</u>　　　Translate into English.

1. اَلصِّرَاطُ الْمُسْتَقِيْمُ
2. عَذَابٌ أَلِيْمٌ
3. بَعُوْضَةٌ صَغِيْرَةٌ
4. رَزَقَهُمُ اللهُ رِزْقًا حَسَنًا
5. بَلَاءٌ عَظِيْمٌ
6. لَيْلَةٌ مُظْلِمَةٌ
7. مَثَلُ كَلِمَةٍ طَيِّبَةٍ كَشَجَرَةٍ طَيِّبَةٍ
8. أَصْلُهَا ثَابِتٌ وَفَرْعُهَا فِي السَّمَاءِ
9. فَتَحَ طَارِقٌ الْقَائِدُ مَدِيْنَةً عَظِيْمَةً وَأَخَذَ حِصْنَهَا مِنْ يَدِ مَلِكٍ عَظِيْمٍ
10. دَخَلَ مُحَمَّدٌ الْفَاتِحُ عَاصِمَةَ الرُّوْمِ

LESSON 9

اَلْأَمْرُ وَالنَّهْيُ
Imperative (Positive Command) &
Prohibitive (Negative Command)

The command is used to demand an action. That verb which contains a command to do something is called أَمْرٌ, for example, 'read!' and 'write!;' while that verb which contains a command to not do something is called نَهْيٌ, as in 'do not go' and 'do not fear.'

Creating أَمْرٌ for the Second Person

أَمْرٌ of any verb is created from its respective فِعْلٌ مُضَارِعٌ. In this lesson, we will study the method of making أَمْرٌ for the second person. This is as follows.

1. First, give a *jazm* to that *seeghah* of فِعْلٌ مُضَارِعٌ, whose أَمْرٌ you wish to create. This means that that *seeghah* which ends with a *dammah*, should have its *dammah* replaced with a *sukoon*, while the *noon* should be dropped from that *seeghah* which ends with a *noon*. The صِيْغَةٌ for جَمْعٌ مُؤَنَّثٌ حَاضِرٌ is an exception to this.[2] Also, in the case of جَمْعٌ مُذَكَّرٌ حَاضِرٌ, an *alif* should be added at the end, after dropping the *noon*.

2. Now, remove the حَرْفُ الْمُضَارِعِ, which in this case is تـ. The *seeghah* should be unreadable.

3. Now, add a هَمْزَةُ الْوَصْلِ at the beginning and give it a *kasrah*.[3]

This process is illustrated in the following table.

---

[2] In fact, this صِيْغَةٌ is one of those words whose ends do not accept any vowel change. Such words are called مَبْنِيٌّ.

[3] *Hamzat al-wasl* appears at the beginning of a word. It is not pronounced when there is a word before the word with a *hamzat al-wasl*. Giving it a *kasrah* is the basic principle. There is more detail to it, and is mentioned later in the lesson.

Lesson 9

Table 9.1
Creating Second Person Imperative In Active Voice (أَمْرٌ حَاضِرٌ مَعْرُوفٌ)
[From Left To Right]

Original *seeghahs* of Second Person فِعْلٌ مُضَارِعٌ	Give *jazm* to the *seeghahs*	Drop the *harf al-mudari‘*	Add a *hamzat al-wasl* at the beginning
تَفْعَلُ	تَفْعَلْ	فْعَلْ	اِفْعَلْ
تَفْعَلَانِ	تَفْعَلَا	فْعَلَا	اِفْعَلَا
تَفْعَلُونَ	تَفْعَلُوا	فْعَلُوا	اِفْعَلُوا
تَفْعَلِينَ	تَفْعَلِي	فْعَلِي	اِفْعَلِي
تَفْعَلَانِ	تَفْعَلَا	فْعَلَا	اِفْعَلَا
تَفْعَلْنَ	تَفْعَلْنَ	فْعَلْنَ	اِفْعَلْنَ

Based upon the above procedure, we get the following *seeghahs* of second person imperative in active voice. These must be memorized.

Table 9.2
Second Person Imperative In Active Voice (أَمْرٌ حَاضِرٌ مَعْرُوفٌ)

Person	Gender	Plurality	English	Arabic
Second Person (حَاضِرٌ)	Masculine (مُذَكَّرٌ)	Singular	(You) Do!	اِفْعَلْ
		Dual	(You) Do!	اِفْعَلَا
		Plural	(You) Do!	اِفْعَلُوا
	Feminine (مُؤَنَّثٌ)	Singular	(You) Do!	اِفْعَلِي
		Dual	(You) Do!	اِفْعَلَا
		Plural	(You) Do!	اِفْعَلْنَ

Before we move on, it would be useful to see how Table 9.2 would be written in Arabic. This is as follows:

Table 9.2a
اَلْأَمْرُ الْحَاضِرُ الْمَعْرُوفُ

اَلصِّيغَةُ	اِسْمُ الصِّيغَةِ
اِفْعَلْ	وَاحِدٌ مُذَكَّرٌ حَاضِرٌ
اِفْعَلَا	تَثْنِيَةٌ مُذَكَّرٌ حَاضِرٌ
اِفْعَلُوا	جَمْعٌ مُذَكَّرٌ حَاضِرٌ
اِفْعَلِي	وَاحِدٌ مُؤَنَّثٌ حَاضِرٌ
اِفْعَلَا	تَثْنِيَةٌ مُؤَنَّثٌ حَاضِرٌ
اِفْعَلْنَ	جَمْعٌ مُؤَنَّثٌ حَاضِرٌ

Examples:

1. From تَفْتَحُ (you are opening/will open), we get اِفْتَحْ (open!).
2. From تَجْلِسُ (you are sitting/will sit), we get اِجْلِسْ (sit!).
3. From تَسْمَعُ (you are hearing/will hear), we get اِسْمَعْ (hear!).
4. From تَضْرِبُ (you are hitting/will hit), we get اِضْرِبْ (hit!).
5. From تَذْهَبُ (you are going/will go), we get اِذْهَبْ (go!).

Creating نَهْيٌ for the Second Person

Like أَمْرٌ, the نَهْيٌ of any verb is also created from its respective فِعْلٌ مُضَارِعٌ. In this lesson, we will study the method of making نَهْيٌ for the second person. It is partially similar to the method given above for أَمْرٌ, but there are also differences. The process is as follows.

1. Like in the case of أَمْرٌ, give a *jazm* to the فِعْلٌ مُضَارِعٌ. This means that that *seeghah* which ends with a *dammah*, should have its *dammah* replaced with a *sukoon*, while the *noon* should be dropped from that *seeghah* which ends with a *noon*. As before, the صِيغَةٌ for جَمْعٌ مُؤَنَّثٌ حَاضِرٌ will be an exception to this. Also, in the case of جَمْعٌ مُذَكَّرٌ حَاضِرٌ, an *alif* should be added at the end, after dropping the *noon*.

Lesson 9

2. Now, instead of removing the حَرْفُ الْمُضَارِعِ, just place a لَا before it. This لَا is a حَرْفُ النَّهْيِ, and is called لَا النَّاهِيَةُ.

This process is illustrated in the following table.

Table 9.3
Creating Second Person Prohibitive In Active Voice (نَهْيٌ حَاضِرٌ مَعْرُوفٌ)
[From Left To Right]

Original *seeghahs* of Second Person فِعْلٌ مُضَارِعٌ	Give *jazm* to the *seeghahs*	Add a *laa al-nahiyah* at the beginning
تَفْعَلُ	تَفْعَلْ	لَا تَفْعَلْ
تَفْعَلَانِ	تَفْعَلَا	لَا تَفْعَلَا
تَفْعَلُونَ	تَفْعَلُوا	لَا تَفْعَلُوا
تَفْعَلِينَ	تَفْعَلِي	لَا تَفْعَلِي
تَفْعَلَانِ	تَفْعَلَا	لَا تَفْعَلَا
تَفْعَلْنَ	تَفْعَلْنَ	لَا تَفْعَلْنَ

Based upon the above procedure, we get the following *seeghahs* of second person prohibitive in active voice. These must be memorized.

Table 9.4
Second Person Prohibitive In Active Voice (نَهْيٌ حَاضِرٌ مَعْرُوفٌ)

Person	Gender	Plurality	English	Arabic
Second Person (حَاضِرٌ)	Masculine (مُذَكَّرٌ)	Singular	(You) Don't do!	لَا تَفْعَلْ
		Dual	(You) Don't do!	لَا تَفْعَلَا
		Plural	(You) Don't do!	لَا تَفْعَلُوا
	Feminine (مُؤَنَّثٌ)	Singular	(You) Don't do!	لَا تَفْعَلِي
		Dual	(You) Don't do!	لَا تَفْعَلَا
		Plural	(You) Don't do!	لَا تَفْعَلْنَ

Again, before we move on, it would be useful to see how Table 9.4 would be written in Arabic. This is as follows:

Table 9.4a
اَلنَّهْيُ الْحَاضِرُ الْمَعْرُوفُ

اَلصِّيغَةُ	اِسْمُ الصِّيغَةِ
لَا تَفْعَلْ	وَاحِدٌ مُذَكَّرٌ حَاضِرٌ
لَا تَفْعَلَا	تَثْنِيَةٌ مُذَكَّرٌ حَاضِرٌ
لَا تَفْعَلُوا	جَمْعٌ مُذَكَّرٌ حَاضِرٌ
لَا تَفْعَلِي	وَاحِدٌ مُؤَنَّثٌ حَاضِرٌ
لَا تَفْعَلَا	تَثْنِيَةٌ مُؤَنَّثٌ حَاضِرٌ
لَا تَفْعَلْنَ	جَمْعٌ مُؤَنَّثٌ حَاضِرٌ

Examples:

1. From تَفْتَحُ (you are opening/will open), we get لَا تَفْتَحْ (do not open!).
2. From تَجْلِسُ (you are sitting/will sit), we get لَا تَجْلِسْ (do not sit!).
3. From تَسْمَعُ (you are hearing/will hear), we get لَا تَسْمَعْ (do not hear!).
4. From تَضْرِبُ (you are hitting/will hit), we get لَا تَضْرِبْ (do not hit!).
5. From تَذْهَبُ (you are going/will go), we get لَا تَذْهَبْ (do not go!).

The vowels (*harakah*) of أَمْرٌ and نَهْيٌ

Many times we find أَمْرٌ to be on the pattern of اِفْعَلْ as in اِسْمَعْ. However, this is not always the case. Sometimes, it follows the اُفْعُلْ pattern as in اُنْصُرْ, and sometimes the اِفْعِلْ pattern as in اِضْرِبْ. The reason behind this difference is that the particular vowel pattern of أَمْرٌ and نَهْيٌ is dependent on the (ع) letter of the وَاحِدٌ مُذَكَّرٌ غَائِبٌ *seeghah* of فِعْلٌ مُضَارِعٌ. The (ع) letter of this فِعْلٌ مُضَارِعٌ وَاحِدٌ مُذَكَّرٌ غَائِبٌ governs the أَمْرٌ in two ways, and نَهْيٌ in one way.

The one way where it governs both أَمْرٌ and نَهْيٌ is the *harakah* of the (ع) letter of أَمْرٌ and نَهْيٌ. Here, the *harakah* has to correspond exactly. Thus, when the (ع) letter of فِعْلٌ مُضَارِعٌ وَاحِدٌ مُذَكَّرٌ غَائِبٌ has a *fathah*, or *kasrah*, or *dammah*, the (ع) letter

Lesson 9

of أَمْر and نَهْي will have the same vowel. For example, in يَسْمَعُ the (ع) letter is (م) and has a *fathah*. Therefore, in its أَمْر and نَهْي forms, the (م) will also get a *fathah*. Its أَمْر will be اِسْمَعْ and its نَهْي will be لَا تَسْمَعْ. In يَضْرِبُ there is a *kasrah* under (ر); therefore, its أَمْر and نَهْي forms will be اِضْرِبْ and لَا تَضْرِبْ respectively. In يَنْصُرُ, there is a *dammah* on (ص); therefore, its أَمْر and نَهْي forms will be اُنْصُرْ and لَا تَنْصُرْ respectively.

The other way in which (ع) letter of فِعْلٌ مُضَارِعٌ governs أَمْر is with respect to the *hamzat al-wasl* of أَمْر. This *hamzat al-wasl* either gets a *kasrah* or a *dammah*. It cannot have a *fathah*. If the (ع) letter of فِعْلٌ مُضَارِعٌ has a *dammah*, the *hamzat al-wasl* of أَمْر will also have a *dammah*. For example, the أَمْر of يَنْصُرُ will be اُنْصُرْ because (ص) is the (ع) letter of فِعْلٌ مُضَارِعٌ and it has a *dammah*. And if the (ع) letter of فِعْلٌ مُضَارِعٌ has a *fathah* or a *kasrah*, then in both cases the *hamzat al-wasl* of أَمْر will get a *kasrah*. For example, the أَمْر of يَسْمَعُ is اِسْمَعْ, and the أَمْر of يَضْرِبُ is اِضْرِبْ.

It should be noted that there is no *hamzat al-wasl* in نَهْي. It is only dependent on the (ع) letter of فِعْلٌ مُضَارِعٌ for the *harakah* on its own (ع) letter.

Word List For Verbs

English (for past tense)	Arabic	
	مَاضٍ	مُضَارِعٌ
he went	ذَهَبَ	يَذْهَبُ
he stopped (someone)	مَنَعَ	يَمْنَعُ
he started	بَدَأَ	يَبْدَأُ
he opened	فَتَحَ	يَفْتَحُ
he searched	بَحَثَ	يَبْحَثُ
he heard	سَمِعَ	يَسْمَعُ
he laughed	ضَحِكَ	يَضْحَكُ
he did, he acted, he worked	عَمِلَ	يَعْمَلُ
he came to know	عَلِمَ	يَعْلَمُ
he played	لَعِبَ	يَلْعَبُ
he accepted	قَبِلَ	يَقْبَلُ

الْأَمْرُ وَالنَّهْيُ

English (for past tense)	Arabic ماضٍ	مُضَارِعٌ
he cooked	طَبَخَ	يَطْبَخُ
he was cautious	حَذِرَ	يَحْذَرُ
he went near, he came near	قَرُبَ	يَقْرُبُ
he became sad	حَزَنَ	يَحْزَنُ
he mocked	هَزَأَ	يَهْزَأُ
he did	فَعَلَ	يَفْعَلُ
he read	قَرَأَ	يَقْرَأُ
he entered	دَخَلَ	يَدْخُلُ
he drank	شَرِبَ	يَشْرَبُ

Word List for Nouns & Particles

English	Arabic Singular	Plural
to	إِلَى	
market	سُوقٌ	
mosque	مَسْجِدٌ	
but, rather, however	بَلْ	
box	صُنْدُوقٌ	
for	لِ	
yourself	نَفْسُكَ	أَنْفُسُكُمْ
a lot	كَثِيرًا	
advice	نَصِيحَةٌ	
mother	أُمٌّ	أُمَّهَاتٌ
with	مَعَ	
doll	دُمْيَةٌ	
ball	كُرَةٌ	
speech	كَلَامٌ	

Lesson 9

English	Arabic	
	Singular	Plural
mirror	مِرْآةٌ	
comb	مِشْطٌ	
meat	لَحْمٌ	
snake	حَيَّةٌ	حَيَّاتٌ
scorpion	عَقْرَبٌ	عَقَارِبُ
cat	قِطَّةٌ	قِطَطٌ
upon, on	عَلَى	
path	صِرَاطٌ	
straight	مُسْتَقِيمٌ	
good	خَيْرٌ	
that	أَنَّ	
all, each	كُلٌّ	
thing	شَيْءٌ	
powerful	قَدِيرٌ	
intercession	شَفَاعَةٌ	
village	قَرْيَةٌ	قُرًى
friend	صَدِيقٌ	
hotel	فُنْدُقٌ	فَنَادِقُ
milk	لَبَنٌ	
door	بَابٌ	
house	بَيْتٌ	
manager; editor	مُدِيرٌ	
newspaper	جَرِيدَةٌ	

Exercise 1: Translate into English

1. اِذْهَبْ
2. لَا تَذْهَبْ
7. لَا تَسْمَعُوا
8. اِضْحَكُوا

3. لَا تَمْنَعُوا		9. اِعْمَلُوا	
4. لَا تَبْدَئِي		10. اِسْتَمَعَ	
5. اِفْتَحِي		11. اِعْلَمَا	
6. لَا تَبْحَثْنَ		12. لَا تَلْعَبَا	

Exercise 2:   Translate into Arabic

1. Don't go (P/M) to the market, but go to the mosque.
2. Open (S/M) the box.
3. Work (D/M) for yourselves.
4. Don't laugh (P/M) a lot.
5. Accept (P/F) the advice of your mothers.
6. Don't (P/M) play with the doll; play (P/M) with the ball.
7. Listen (S/M) to the speech of Allah.
8. Don't (S/F) play with the mirror and the comb; cook (S/F) the meat.
9. Be cautious (P/F) of the snake and the scorpion.
10. Don't (D/F) go near the ball; play (D/F) with this cat.

Exercise 3:   Translate into English.

1. لَا تَحْزَنْ عَلَيْهِمْ
2. لَا تَهْزَءُوا وَلَا تَضْحَكُوا
3. اِفْعَلُوا الْخَيْرَ
4. اِقْرَئِي وَلَا تَلْعَبِي
5. اِعْلَمُوا أَنَّ اللهَ عَلَى كُلِّ شَيْءٍ قَدِيرٌ
6. اِقْبَلُوا الشَّفَاعَةَ
7. اُدْخُلُوا هٰذِهِ الْقَرْيَةَ
8. اِذْهَبُوا مَعَ صَدِيقِكُمْ إِلَى الْفُنْدُقِ وَاشْرَبُوا اللَّبَنَ مَعَهُ
9. اِفْتَحُوا بَابَ الْبَيْتِ وَاذْهَبُوا إِلَى مُدِيرِ الْجَرِيدَةِ

LESSON 10

اَلْوَاحِدُ، اَلتَّثْنِيَةُ، اَلْجَمْعُ
Singular, Dual, Plural

We have seen in the previous lessons that verb forms are sometimes single, sometimes dual, and sometimes plural.[4] Similarly, nouns can also be single, dual and plural. For example, مُؤْمِنٌ means 'one believer,' مُؤْمِنَانِ means 'two believers,' and مُؤْمِنُوْنَ means 'three or more believers.' Below, we give the rules for duals and plurals of nouns.

تَثْنِيَةٌ – **Dual**: It is formed by placing at the end of a singular (وَاحِدٌ) one of the following:

- An أَلِفٌ preceded by a *fathah* and followed by a نُوْنٌ with a *kasrah* i.e. [ـَانِ] for the state of رَفْعٌ.

  e.g.   رَجُلَانِ   two men

- A يَاءٌ preceded by a *fathah* and a نُوْنٌ with a *kasrah* i.e. [ـَيْنِ] for the states of نَصْبٌ and جَرٌّ.

  e.g.   رَجُلَيْنِ   two men

جَمْعٌ – **Plural**: It is formed by placing at the end of a singular (وَاحِدٌ) one of the following:[5]

- A وَاوٌ preceded by a *dammah* and followed by a نُوْنٌ with a *fathah* i.e. [ـُوْنَ] for the state of رَفْعٌ.

  e.g.   مُسْلِمُوْنَ   Muslims

- A يَاءٌ preceded by a *kasrah* and followed by a نُوْنٌ with a *fathah* i.e. [ـِيْنَ] for the states of نَصْبٌ and جَرٌّ.

  e.g.   مُسْلِمِيْنَ   Muslims

---

[4] It should be remembered that when the verb forms are dual or plural, it is not the action that is dual or plural. The action taking place is only one. It is only the doers of the action who are two or more.
[5] There is more detail to it, which can be studied in more advanced books.

Lesson 10

For the ease of the students, a chart showing مُسْلِمٌ and its dual and plural forms in each of the different states is given below.

Table 10.1
Singular, Dual, and Plural

	Singular (اَلْوَاحِدُ)	Dual (اَلتَّثْنِيَةُ)	Plural (اَلْجَمْعُ)
In the state of رَفْعٌ	مُسْلِمٌ	مُسْلِمَانِ	مُسْلِمُوْنَ
In the state of نَصْبٌ	مُسْلِمًا	مُسْلِمَيْنِ	مُسْلِمِيْنَ
In the state of جَرٌّ	مُسْلِمٍ	مُسْلِمَيْنِ	مُسْلِمِيْنَ

Examples:

1. Two men went to the market.
   ذَهَبَ رَجُلَانِ إِلَى السُّوْقِ

2. The scholars gave a speech in the mosque.
   خَطَبَ الْعَالِمُوْنَ فِي الْمَسْجِدِ

3. Khalid helped two oppressed persons.
   نَصَرَ خَالِدٌ مَظْلُوْمَيْنِ

4. Naseer hit the oppressors.
   ضَرَبَ نَصِيْرٌ اَلظَّالِمِيْنَ

5. I wrote with two pens.
   كَتَبْتُ بِقَلَمَيْنِ

6. A man from amongst the believers came.
   جَاءَ رَجُلٌ مِنَ الْمُؤْمِنِيْنَ

Note: The نُوْنٌ of dual and plural is dropped when it appears at the end of *mudaaf*. For example,

1. قَلَمَا زَيْدٍ (Zayd's two pens)

   This was originally قَلَمَانِ زَيْدٍ but the نُوْنٌ was dropped because it appeared at the end of *mudaaf*.

2. فَرَسَا رَجُلٍ (a man's two horses)

   This was originally فَرَسَانِ رَجُلٍ but the نُوْنٌ was dropped because it appeared at the end of *mudaaf*.

3. مُسْلِمُوْ مِصْرَ (Muslims of Egypt)

This was originally مُسْلِمُوْنَ مِصْرَ but the نُوْنٌ was dropped because it appeared at the end of *mudaaf*.

4. طَالِبُوْ عِلْمٍ (seekers of knowledge)

This was originally طَالِبُوْنَ عِلْمٍ but the نُوْنٌ was dropped because it appeared at the end of *mudaaf*.

Word List for Verbs

English (for past tense)	Arabic مَاضٍ	مُضَارِعٌ
he ordered	أَمَرَ	يَأْمُرُ
he wrote	كَتَبَ	يَكْتُبُ
he ate	أَكَلَ	يَأْكُلُ
he cut	قَطَعَ	يَقْطَعُ
he hit	ضَرَبَ	يَضْرِبُ
he took	أَخَذَ	يَأْخُذُ
he studied	دَرَسَ	يَدْرُسُ
he cooked	طَبَخَ	يَطْبَخُ
he read	قَرَأَ	يَقْرَأُ
he filled	مَلَأَ	يَمْلَأُ
he imprisoned	حَبَسَ	يَحْبِسُ
he forgave	غَفَرَ	يَغْفِرُ

Word List for Nouns

English	Arabic Singular	Plural
preacher	وَاعِظٌ	وَاعِظُوْنَ
book	كِتَابٌ	كُتُبٌ
believer	مُؤْمِنٌ	مُؤْمِنُوْنَ
bread	خُبْزٌ	أَخْبَازٌ

Lesson 10

English	Arabic	
	Singular	Plural
tree	شَجَرَةٌ	
boy	وَلَدٌ	
umbrella	مِظَلَّةٌ	
year	سَنَةٌ، عَامٌ	سِنُوْنَ، أَعْوَامٌ
worshipper	عَابِدٌ	عُبَّادٌ
a fish	سَمَكَةٌ	
notebook	كُرَّاسَةٌ	
house	بَيْتٌ	
female servant, maid	خَادِمَةٌ	
jar	جَرَّةٌ	
uncle (maternal)	خَالٌ	
thief	سَارِقٌ	سَارِقُوْنَ
jail, prison	سِجْنٌ	
guidance	هُدًى	
pious, God-fearing	مُتَّقٍ (الْمُتَّقِيْ)	مُتَّقُوْنَ (الْمُتَّقُوْنَ)
successful; prosperous	مُفْلِحٌ	مُفْلِحُوْنَ
corrupt	مُفْسِدٌ	مُفْسِدُوْنَ
we	نَحْنُ	
peacemaker	مُصْلِحٌ	مُصْلِحُوْنَ
oppressor	ظَالِمٌ	ظَالِمُوْنَ
punishment	عَذَابٌ	
painful	أَلِيْمٌ	
disbeliever, infidel	كَافِرٌ	كَافِرُوْنَ
humiliating, disgraceful	مُهِيْنٌ	
with	مَعَ	
patient	صَابِرٌ	صَابِرُوْنَ
all praise	الْحَمْدُ	

English	Arabic	
	Singular	Plural
Lord	رَبٌّ	
world	عَالَمٌ	عَالَمُوْنَ
blessing, grace (of Allah Most High)	صَلوٰةٌ	
peace	سَلَامٌ	
upon, on	عَلَى	
master; chief	سَيِّدٌ	
messenger	مُرْسَلٌ	مُرْسَلُوْنَ
seal; ring	خَاتَمٌ	خَوَاتَمُ
prophet	نَبِيٌّ	نَبِيُّوْنَ
family	آلٌ	
companion	صَاحِبٌ	أَصْحَابٌ
all	أَجْمَعُ	أَجْمَعُوْنَ

Exercise 1:   Translate into Arabic

1. I ordered the preachers.
2. They (P/M) wrote a book for the believers.
3. They (P/F) ate the bread.
4. You (P/M) cut the tree.
5. She hit two boys and she took the umbrellas.
6. You (P/F) will study for two years.
7. You (S/F) will cook for the worshippers.
8. You (S/M) ate a fish, but I ate two fish.
9. She wrote two notebooks and you (P/M) read two books.
10. The house's maid cooked bread and she filled two jars.
11. Khalid's uncle (maternal) imprisoned the thieves in the jail.

Exercise 2:   Translate into English

1. اَلْقُرْآنُ هُدًى لِلْمُتَّقِيْنَ
2. اَلْمُؤْمِنُوْنَ مُفْلِحُوْنَ
3. قَالَ الْمُفْسِدُوْنَ: نَحْنُ مُصْلِحُوْنَ

Lesson 10

4. لِلظَّلِمِيْنَ عَذَابٌ أَلِيْمٌ
5. لِلْكَافِرِيْنَ عَذَابٌ مُهِيْنٌ
6. اَللهُ مَعَ الصَّابِرِيْنَ
7. اَللهُ يَغْفِرُ لِلْمُؤْمِنِيْنَ
8. اَلْحَمْدُ لِلهِ رَبِّ الْعَلَمِيْنَ
9. اَلصَّلَاةُ وَالسَّلَامُ عَلَى سَيِّدِ الْمُرْسَلِيْنَ خَاتَمِ النَّبِيِّيْنَ مُحَمَّدٍ وَعَلَى أَلِهِ وَأَصْحَابِهِ أَجْمَعِيْنَ

Made in the USA
Las Vegas, NV
18 January 2025

16599691R00090